the Vocabulary of Success

Also by C. Edward Good

Mightier than the Sword—Powerful Writing in the Legal Profession
A Grammar Book for You and I . . . Oops, Me!

Other Titles in the Capital Ideas Series

Be Heard the First Time: The Woman's Guide to Powerful Speaking
by Susan D. Miller

Family Writes: Parenting with Pens, Pencils, and PCs
by Joel Epstein and Peggy Epstein

The New Talk Power: The Mind-Body Way to Speak Like a Pro
by Natalie H. Rogers

Tough Questions—Good Answers: Taking Control of Any Interview
by Thomas F. Calcagni

the Vocabulary *of* Success

403
words smart people should know

C. Edward Good

Capital Ideas Series
CAPITAL BOOKS, INC.
Sterling, Virginia

Capital Books, Inc.
P.O. Box 605
Herndon, Virginia 20172-0605

ISBN 13: 978-1-933102-66-5

Library of Congress Cataloging-in-Publication Data
Good, C. Edward.
The vocabulary of success : 403 words smart people should know / C. Edward Good. — 1st ed.
p. cm. — (Capital ideas series)
Includes bibliographical references.
ISBN 978-1-933102-66-5 (alk. paper)
1. Vocabulary. 2. English language—Usage. I. Title. II. Series.

PE1449.G574 2008
428.1—dc22

2008034128

Printed in the United States of America on acid-free paper that meets the American National Standards Institute Z39-48 Standard.

First Edition

10 9 8 7 6 5 4 3 2 1

For Margaret with love and gratitude.

For Lucy, Natalie, Charles, and Caitlin.
Thanks for changing and improving my life.

Contents

Take This Test

Pick the correct definition of the following words:

1. disingenuous

   a. insincere

   b. dishonest

   c. cranky

2. forgo

   a. to give up

   b. to go before

   c. to reach an inevitable conclusion

3. travesty

   a. a grotesque imitation

   b. a grave miscarriage of justice

   c. an intricately patterned piece of cloth

Did you pick the correct definition? Read the following Preface. Somewhere in it we've provided the answers.

Preface

When reading, watching TV, or surfing the Internet, I often come across words whose meanings escape me. "But I'm smart," I would think to myself. "I'm supposed to know these words." Then, making sure no one was watching, I'd make furtive trips to the dictionary.

My mind went back way too many years, to those halcyon days of my youth when my mother forced me to read a book called *Word Power*, or something like that. Her exercise—"Learn and use one word each day"—worked, for I managed to cobble together a reasonable performance on the SAT and then matriculate first at the University of North Carolina and then, later, at the University of Virginia School of Law.

My mother loved language and grammar, as did my two no-nonsense English teachers at Kaiser Junior High School in Greensboro, North Carolina—Mrs. Hazelman and Miss Hamrick. Their combined influence—no, power—seeped into me at a young age and ended up guiding my career. I eschewed the practice of law, choosing instead to educate myself in grammar and style, declare myself an expert, and launch a life-long crusade of teaching lawyers and other professionals how to write like normal people.

Now I serve as the Writer-in-Residence at Finnegan, Henderson, Farabow, Garrett & Dunner, LLP, the world's largest law firm practicing intellectual-property law. I provide ongoing training programs not only to the firm's lawyers and staff but also to many of the firm's clients. Clients have sponsored training programs in effective writing in Shanghai, Taipei, Brussels, Dijon, and cities throughout the United States.

Along the way, on many nights and weekends, I managed to pen some works, chief among them *A Grammar Book for You and I . . . Oops, Me!* Then, not to be left behind in this Age of the Internet, I took the *Oops Me* book and turned it into a Clickable Help System for Writers. It's called GrammaRight. You can read about it on my website: Grammar.com.

My dear friend, neighbor, and publisher, Kathleen Hughes, urged me to write another book. I thought back to my furtive trips to the dictionary and suggested, "How about a book of words?"

"What words?" she asked.

"Words smart people should know," I responded.

So I scoured word lists from a variety of sources, picking out those that often appear in literature, history, philosophy, and modern media. Beginning with a list of more than 5,000, I narrowed it down to 403. Not 404. Not 402. But 403.

Then I had an idea: I'll not only define the words but find examples of their usage by the world's top writers.

So in these pages, you'll read passages of Nathaniel Hawthorne using **ascetic**, Andrea Dworkin using **premise**, P.J. O'Rourke using **officious**, John Milton using **harbinger**, Charles Dickens using **loquacious**, Leo Tolstoy using **expiate**, and the list goes on and on.

I hope you enjoy learning—relearning?—the 403 words. And I know you'll enjoy reading the examples of usage. Oh, and by the way, the correct answer for each of the Take This Test words is "a."

And finally, a note of thanks: To my wife Margaret, thank you. Thank you for putting up with my late nights at the computer keyboard and with all the rest of me.

Signed: YLHABF.

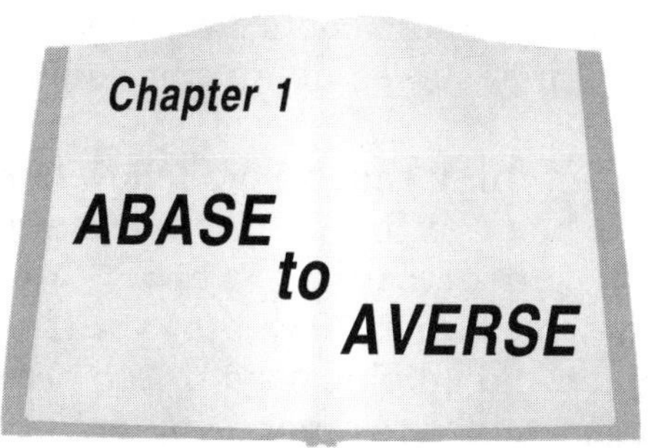

1. abase

verb

To deprive of esteem, to diminish a person's self-worth or effectiveness; to degrade or demean; to humble, humiliate, mortify; to bring low, take down a peg.

> When metastases appeared, men were castrated, since testosterone seemed to promote cancer growth. Does this mean that urological surgeons were, consciously or subconsciously, acting out as alpha males to dominate and **abase** vulnerable men of the tribe?
>
> —Jerome Groopman
> "The Sexual Politics of Cancer"
> *New York Times*, January 9, 2000

2. abject

adjective

Sunk to a low condition, miserable, degraded, without self-respect, of the lowest kind.

Note: Often used in the cliché, *abject poverty*, where *abject* really only serves as an intensifier.

> I do not think that an old fellow like me need have been sitting here to try and prevent your entertaining **abject** notions of yourselves, and talking of yourselves in an **abject** and ignoble way: but to prevent there being by chance among you any such young men as, after recognising their kindred to the Gods, and their bondage in these chains of the body and its manifold necessities, should desire to cast them off as burdens too grievous to be borne, and depart to their true kindred. This is the struggle in which your Master and Teacher, were he worthy of the name, should be engaged.
>
> —Epictetus
> *The Golden Sayings of Epictetus*

3. abjure

verb

To recant; to repudiate under oath; to disavow a stance previously written or said; to renounce irrevocably.

> 2. *Resolved,* That we the citizens of Mecklenburg County, do hereby *dissolve the political bands which have connected* us to the Mother Country, and hereby *absolve* ourselves *from all allegiance to the British Crown,* and **abjure** *all political connection,* contract, or association, with that Nation, who have wantonly trampled on our rights

> and liberties—and inhumanly shed the innocent blood of American patriots at Lexington.
>
> —The Mecklenburg Declaration of Independence
> American Historical Documents, (1000–1904)
> The Harvard Classics, (1909–14).

4. abeyance

noun

A state of suspension or temporary inaction; the condition of being temporarily set aside or held in suspension, as in *They held the program in abeyance.* In law, a condition of undetermined ownership as when a property right has yet to be assigned.

> And then she lived, with Mrs. Osmond, under the influence of a pleasant surprise; she was constantly expecting that Isabel would "look down" upon her and she as constantly saw this operation postponed. She asked herself when it would begin; not that she cared much; but she wondered what kept it in **abeyance**.
>
> —Henry James
> *The Portrait of a Lady* (1908)

5. abominate

verb

To dislike strongly; to regard with loathing; to execrate.

> Now is as good a time as ever to revisit the history of the Crusades, or the sorry history of partition in Kashmir, or the woes of the Chechens and Kosovars. But the bombers of Manhattan represent fascism with an Islamic face, and there's no point in any euphemism about it. What they **abominate** about "the West," to put it in a phrase, is not what Western liberals don't like and can't defend about their own system, but what they do like about it and must defend: its emancipated women, its scientific inquiry, its separation of religion from the state.
>
> —Christopher Hitchens
> "Against Rationalization"
> *The Nation*, October 8, 2001

6. abrogate

verb

To abolish by official means; to annul by an authoritative act; to repeal, as in *to abrogate a law*; to put an end to.

> The new crusade to render socialism irrevocable has raised the temperature further. Yet the balance of the past decade already may have begun to totter. Former President Jimmy Carter's visit, which spotlighted the Varela Project, may have tipped the international balance. Now the world is asking more forcefully: Why doesn't Cuba change? Decline in tourism and remittances after Sept. 11, uncertainties in oil supplies and the closing of nearly half

the island's sugar mills, all manifest a new economic downturn.

Rhetoric aside, the Bush administration has not really applied a markedly harsher policy. Congress still could seek to lift travel restrictions and allow U.S. credits for food purchases. That, however, would be less likely if Castro carries out recent threats to close the U.S. Interests Section and **abrogate** the migration agreement.

—Marifeli Perez-Stable
"Cuba's Regime at a Crossroads"
Miami Herald, July 11, 2002

7. abstemious

adjective

A state of self-denial or abstinence, regarding the use (usually overuse) of food or drink.

When [Marcus Aurelius Antoninus (121–180)] was eleven years old, he assumed the dress of philosophers, something plain and coarse, became a hard student, and lived a most laborious, **abstemious** life, even so far as to injure his health. Finally, he abandoned poetry and rhetoric for philosophy, and he attached himself to the sect of the Stoics. But he did not neglect the study of law, which was a useful preparation for the high place which he was designed to fill. His teacher was L. Volusianus Maecianus, a distinguished jurist. We must suppose that he learned the Roman discipline of arms, which was a necessary part of the education of a man who

> afterwards led his troops to battle against a warlike race.
>
> —George Long
> *M. Aurelius Antoninus* (1909–14)

8. abstruse

adjective

Having to do with matters difficult to comprehend.

> My mind rebels at stagnation. Give me problems, give me work, give me the most **abstruse** cryptogram, or the most intricate analysis, and I am in my own proper atmosphere. I can dispense then with artificial stimulants. But I abhor the dull routine of existence. I crave for mental exaltation.
>
> —Sir Arthur Conan Doyle
> *The Sign of Four* (1890)

9. acumen

noun

Quickness of intellectual insight, or discernment; keenness of judgment, insight, discrimination.

Note: The older pronunciation stresses the second syllable. The modern pronunciation stresses the first syllable.

> Eugene Meyer's enlightened editorial policies and his business **acumen** began to turn the *Washington Post* around. In the first ten years after he took over, circulation tripled to 162,000 and advertising soared from 4

million to 12 million lines. However, The Post continued to lose money.

—"History & Leadership"
The Washington Post Company
Washpostco.com

10. adduce

verb

To bring forward evidence in an argument; to cite as pertinent or even conclusive. As shown below, often used in legal proceedings:

> President Clinton, through undersigned counsel, hereby moves the Court pursuant to Federal Rule of Civil Procedure 56(b) to enter judgment for him on all claims in plaintiff's First Amended Complaint. As fully demonstrated below and in the accompanying Memorandum and Exhibits, plaintiff has failed to **adduce** evidence showing the existence of essential elements of each of her claims. Therefore, President Clinton is entitled to judgment as a matter of law.

—Former President Clinton's Motion for Summary Judgment
Jones v. Clinton
washingtonpost.com, February 18, 1998

11. aggrandize

noun

Aggrandizement: the act of increasing the size or importance of something or somebody.

verb

Aggrandize: to widen or increase in size or intensity; to make great or greater in wealth, power, honor, or rank; to make something appear greater.

Note: Both the noun and verb are often used with the prefix self-.

> The historian's job is to **aggrandize**, promoting accident to inevitability and innocuous circumstance to portent.
>
> —Peter Conrad
> *The Art of the City* (1984)

12. alacrity

noun

A state of cheerful willingness, readiness, or promptness; liveliness or briskness, as in *He accepted the promotion with alacrity.*

> I have not that **alacrity** of spirit
> Nor cheer of mind that I was wont to have.
>
> —William Shakespeare
> *Richard III* (1591)

13. amenable

adjective

Willing or ready to answer, serve, agree, yield, or act; agreeable, tractable; legally responsible or answerable, as in *She was amenable for her husband's debt.*

Despite the document's adoption, however, it was clear that the most contentious issue of the talks—setting hard emissions caps for individual countries—would simply be pushed into the future in anticipation of the election of a new U.S. president who might be more **amenable** to restrictions.

—Alan Zarembo and Thomas H. Maugh II
"After-Hours Deal at Climate Talks"
Los Angeles Times, December 15, 2007

14. anachronism

noun

Anything or anyone not in the correct historical or chronological time; an error in the assignment of a date or time to a person, thing, or event, as in *To describe Mozart in the 19th century is an anachronism.*

In a consultation room at San Francisco General Hospital, Warren Ratcliffe rolls up the leg of his jeans to display an **anachronism**. Purplish brown, leech-shaped splotches cover his left shin and calf. They exist also, he says, on his stomach and chest, and he fears they might appear on his hands and face, where clothing won't obscure them.

Kaposi's sarcoma, once the familiar and portentous calling card of the deadly AIDS epidemic, has all but disappeared over the last decade, during which multidrug "cocktail" therapy has drained HIV of much of its ferocity and returned many patients

> to normal lives. The markings on Ratcliffe's skin, however, tell of a grim exception.
>
> —James Ricci
> "The Ones HIV Left in Limbo"
> *Los Angeles Times*, January 19, 2006

15. anathema

noun

A person or thing loathed, hated, or detested; a curse or execration, as in *This topic is anathema to him.*

Note: The plural is *anathemas.*

> Give me your **anathema**.
> Speak new damnations on my head.
> The evening mist in the hills is soft.
> The boulders on the road say communion.
> The farm dogs look out of their eyes and keep thoughts from the corn cribs.
> Dirt of the reeling earth holds horseshoes.
> The rings in the whiffletree count their secrets.
> Come on, you.
>
> —Carl Sandburg
> *Smoke and Steel* (1922)

16. anecdote, antidote

Anecdote:
noun

A brief account of an interesting or even amusing event or incident.

> When the ladies removed after dinner Elizabeth ran up to her sister, and seeing her well guarded from cold, attended her into the drawing-room, where she was welcomed by her two friends with many professions of pleasure; and Elizabeth had never seen them so agreeable as they were during the hour which passed before the gentlemen appeared. Their powers of conversation were considerable. They could describe an entertainment with accuracy, relate an **anecdote** with humour, and laugh at their acquaintance with spirit.
>
> —Jane Austen
> *Pride and Prejudice* (1813)

Antidote:
noun

A remedy given to counteract poison or a disease; often used metaphorically, as in *Forbidding television in the home is often a good antidote to teenage drug abuse.*

> To Sergey Ivanovitch the country meant on one hand rest from work, on the other a valuable **antidote** to the corrupt influences of town, which he took with satisfaction and a sense of its utility. To Konstantin Levin the country was good first because it afforded a field for labour, of the usefulness of which there could be no doubt. To Sergey Ivanovitch the country was particularly good, because there it was possible and fitting to do nothing.
>
> —Leo Tolstoy
> *Anna Karenin* (1877)

verb

To counteract with an *antidote*, as in *To save her child, the mother antidoted the sting with baking soda.*

17. antediluvian

adjective

Of or pertaining to the times, things, events before the great flood in the days of Noah; something old-fashioned, antiquated, out-of-date.

> "And is it true the younger Vlassiev girl's to marry Topov?"
> "Yes, they say it's quite a settled thing."
> "I wonder at the parents! They say it's a marriage for love."
> "For love? What **antediluvian** notions you have! Can one talk of love in these days?" said the ambassador's wife.
>
> —Leo Tolstoy
> *Anna Karenin* (1877)

18. aphorism

noun

A terse saying that embodies a general truth, as in (with apologies to Lord Acton) *Power corrupts and Power Point corrupts absolutely.*

Note: In *The World in a Phrase*, his 2005 history of the form, James Geary laid down his "Five Laws of the **Aphorism**: It Must Be Brief, It Must Be Personal, It Must Be Definitive, It Must Be Philosophical, and It Must Have A Twist."

Need some examples? Here are three, honestly chosen at random, from *Geary's Guide to the World's Great Aphorists*:

> "Between two evils, I always pick the one I never tried before."
>
> —Mae West
>
> "To live is to lose ground."
>
> —E. M. Cioran
>
> "The only things one never regrets are one's mistakes."
>
> —Oscar Wilde
>
> —Michael Dirda, *Geary's Guide to the World's Greatest Aphorists*
> *Washington Post*, October 21, 2007

19. apposite

adjective

Appropriate, well-suited, apt, relevant, suitable. The opposite is *inapposite*, often used by lawyers to put down opponents' arguments.

> Like most writers, [Millard] Kaufman is an avid reader; he calls F. Scott Fitzgerald's "The Great Gatsby" a "masterpiece" and said he rereads it once a year. His highest praise, however, goes to Charles Dickens' "Bleak House." "I think it's the best novel ever written in the English language," he said. "Dickens is unbelievable—his choice of the **apposite** word and his humor—and it's so interesting because he's so good at writing but he made such a mess of his own life."
>
> —Steffie Nelson
> "Screenwriter and Mr. Magoo

> Co-creator Pens His Debut Novel at Age 90"
> *Los Angeles Times*, October 31, 2007

20. approbation

noun

Approval, commendation, official sanction.

> Superstars strive for **approbation**; heroes walk alone. Superstars crave consensus; heroes define themselves by the judgment of a future they see it as their task to bring about. Superstars seek success in a technique for eliciting support; heroes pursue success as the outgrowth of inner values.
>
> —Henry Kissinger
> Review of *Churchill* by Norman Rose
> *New York Times Book Review*, July 16, 1995

21. apostasy, apostate

noun

Apostasy: a total departure from one's religious, political, or personal beliefs and principles.

Apostate: a person who forsakes his or her religious, political, or personal beliefs and principles.

Note: *Apostate* can also be used as an adjective to mean not faithful to one's religious, political, or personal beliefs and principles.

> Mr. Rahman, [who converted to Christianity], stands accused of **apostasy**, or ridda, the act of renouncing one's faith. **Apostasy** is a

grave sin in Islam, and according to classical Shariah, it warrants a punishment of execution. But Islamic laws, including those governing the treatment of **apostates**, were developed as early as the eighth century against a vastly different political and social backdrop.

—Andrea Elliott
"In Kabul, a Test for Shariah"
New York Times, March 26, 2006

22. arrogate

verb

To take, demand, or claim, especially presumptuously or without reasons or grounds.

This second source of men, while yet but few,
. . .
Shall lead their lives, and multiply apace,
. . .
Shall spend their days in joy unblamed, and dwell
Long time in peace, by families and tribes,
Under paternal rule, till one shall rise,
Of proud, ambitious heart, who, not content
With fair equality, fraternal state,
Will **arrogate** dominion undeserved
Over his brethren, and quite dispossess
Concord and law of Nature from the Earth—
Hunting (and men, not beasts, shall be his game)
With war and hostile snare such as refuse
Subjection to his empire tyrannous.

—John Milton
Paradise Lost (1667)

23. ascetic

adjective

Given to severe self-denial and practicing excessive abstinence and devotion.

> Hester sought not to acquire anything beyond a subsistence, of the plainest and most **ascetic** description, for herself, and a simple abundance for her child. Her own dress was of the coarsest materials and the most sombre hue, with only that one ornament—the scarlet letter—which it was her doom to wear.
>
> —Nathaniel Hawthorne
> *The Scarlet Letter* (1850)

24. askance

adverb

Usually describes the act of looking or glancing; with suspicion or mistrust, as in *He looked askance at his boss, who seemed to bring bad tidings.*

> "Do you suppose he can possibly recover?" said Levin, watching a slender tress at the back of her round little head that was continually hidden when she passed the comb through the front.
>
> "I asked the doctor; he said he couldn't live more than three days. But can they be sure? I'm very glad, any way, that I persuaded him," she said, looking **askance** at her husband through her hair. "Anything is possible," she added with that peculiar,

rather sly expression that was always in her face when she spoke of religion.

—Leo Tolstoy
Anna Karenin (1877)

25. assiduous

adjective

Constant or unremitting activity, as in *assiduous exercise*; constant in application or effort; diligent or persevering, as in *an assiduous medical student.*

> Callendar's concern was pursued in the 1950s by numerous American scientists, including oceanographer Roger Revelle, a one-time commander in the U.S. Navy Hydrographic Office, who helped his colleague Charles David Keeling find funds to implement a systematic monitoring program. By the 1960s, Keeling's **assiduous** measurements at Mauna Loa Observatory in Hawaii demonstrated conclusively that atmospheric carbon dioxide was, indeed, steadily rising.
>
> —Naomi Oreskes
> "The Long Consensus on Climate Change"
> *Washington Post*, February 1, 2007

26. assuage

verb

To cause to be less harsh, severe, or violent, usually in reference to appetite, pain, disease, or excitement, as in *She assuaged the pain of her terminally ill patient.*

> As psychologists begin to explore the boundaries of regret, marketers have already begun to exploit the emotion in promotions of products ranging from greeting cards to flowers to automobiles.
>
> —Barry Meier
> "The Regret Business: Marketers Tool Products to **Assuage** Feelings"
> *New York Times*, January 2, 1994

27. astringent

noun

A substance that contracts canals or tissues in the body; in cosmetics, a substance that cleans the skin and constricts the pores.

adjective

> Harsh in disposition or character; in medicine, constricting or contracting.
>
> About the size and shape of an average tomato, the seedless Fuyu has red-orange skin and when sliced displays a beautiful star pattern. The flavor is sweet, rich and not the least bit **astringent**.
>
> —Walter Nicholls,
> "From the Tropics to the Grocery Store"
> *Washington Post*, December 19, 2007

28. audacious

adjective

Fearless, bold, daring, as in *an audacious explorer;*

extremely original or inventive, as in *his audacious vision for improving the tax laws.*

> The Bush administration's **audacious** plan to rebuild Iraq envisions a sweeping overhaul of Iraqi society within a year of a war's end, but leaves much of the work to private U.S. companies.
>
> —Neil King, Jr.
> "Bush Has an **Audacious** Plan to Rebuild Iraq Within a Year"
> *Wall Street Journal*, March 17, 2003

29. augur

verb

Note: Used as either a transitive verb (where the verb requires an object) or an intransitive verb (where the verb does not require an object). Also note the spelling. The noun *auger* is a drill.

Augur (transitive): to divine, predict, or prognosticate an occurrence, as in *Increased exports augured a decline in the trade deficit.*

Augur (intransitive): to bode or to be a sign, as in *The approaching storm augured ill for those living along the bank of the already flooded river.*

> The strong opening weekend for *Spider-Man 3* may **augur** well for a season in which more than a dozen big-budget sequels are set to come barreling forth, promising what some

> experts say could be a record-breaking summer for the movie industry.
>
> —Sharon Waxman
> "*Spider-Man 3* Box Office Bodes Well for Summer"
> *New York Times*, May 7, 2007

30. avarice

noun

An unquenchable desire for riches; a miserly desire.

> By **avarice** and selfishness, and a groveling habit, from which none of us is free, of regarding the soil as property, or the means of acquiring property chiefly, the landscape is deformed, husbandry is degraded with us, and the farmer leads the meanest of lives. He knows Nature but as a robber.
>
> —Henry David Thoreau
> "The Bean-Field"
> *Walden* (1854)

31. aver

verb

To assert or affirm with confidence; to declare in a preemptory or positive manner. In law, to allege something as a fact, often followed by a *that* clause, as in *The plaintiff averred that defendant was negligent.*

> So General Grant, after circumambiating the world, has arrived home again—landed in San Francisco yesterday, from the ship City of Tokio from Japan. What a man he is! what

a history! what an illustration—his life—of the capacities of that American individuality common to us all. Cynical critics are wondering "what the people can see in Grant" to make such a hubbub about. They **aver** (and it is no doubt true) that he has hardly the average of our day's literary and scholastic culture, and absolutely no pronounced genius or conventional eminence of any sort. Correct: but he proves how an average western farmer, mechanic, boatman, carried by tides of circumstances, perhaps caprices, into a position of incredible military or civic responsibilities, . . . may steer his way fitly and steadily through them all, carrying the country and himself with credit year after year—command over a million armed men—fight more than fifty heavy battles—rule for eight years a land larger than all the kingdoms of Europe combined—and then, retiring, quietly (with a cigar in his mouth) make the promenade of the whole world, through its courts and coteries, and kings and czars and mikados, and splendidest glitters and etiquettes, as phlegmatically as he ever walked the portico of a Missouri hotel after dinner.

—Walt Whitman
Prose Works
September 28, 1879

32. averse

adjective

Strongly disinclined, a strong feeling of opposition, as in *She was averse to taking the risk.*

Note: Often used with the negative *not*, as in *I am not averse to having yet another glass of fine pinot noir.*

> I've never downloaded a podcast, but I'm not **averse** to doing so. It's another thing I'm not up on.
>
> —Eric Zorn
> *Chicago Tribune*, September 6, 2007
> Quoting Mark Caro,
> pop-culture writer and blogger

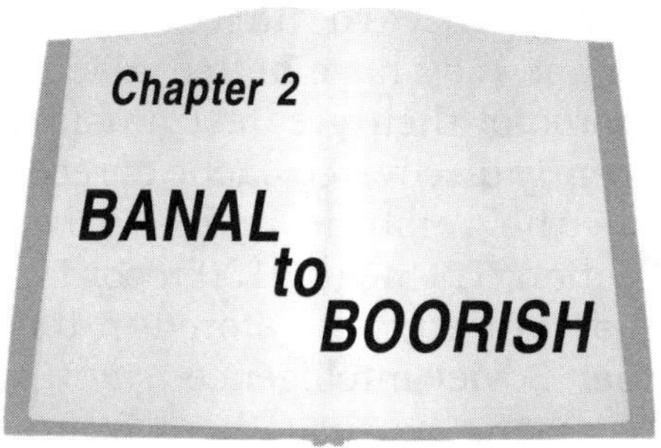

33. banal

adjective

Drearily commonplace, hackneyed, trite, lacking in originality.

> If you killed off Lizzie McGuire's entire family and sent her to live with an evil stepmother and two stepsisters in the Valley, you'd have the basic setup for "A Cinderella Story," the **banal**, contemporary update of the popular fairy tale that stars Hilary Duff, best known as the Disney Channel poster girl.
>
> —Kevin Crust
> Film Review of *A Cinderella Story* (2004)
> *Los Angeles Times*, July 16, 2004

34. belie

verb

To misrepresent, to show to be false; to refute, disprove, gainsay. Often used to show an action directly contrary to the true situation, as in *His shaking hands belied his calm smile and voice.*

> Hitler's outward hatred for Jews and Russians may have **belied** a secret passion for some of their greatest musical works, if a recently discovered cache of records proves to be the remains of his private music collection. The nearly 100 records, now worn and scratched, were stored in the attic of a former Soviet intelligence agent, who left a note saying he took them from the Reich Chancellery after the fall of Berlin in 1945.
>
> —Michael Schwirtz
> "Music Found in Moscow May Be Hitler's"
> *Herald Tribune*, August 7, 2007

35. bemoan

verb

To lament; to express grief or distress over; to regard with disapproval or regret.

> Back in May, Sen. Hillary Rodham Clinton publicly admonished young folks for thinking of work as a "four-letter word," prompting a shaming from her own overachieving 27-year-old daughter. Six and a half months closer to the election, it appears Clinton now thinks it strategically unwise to insult an entire voting bloc that leans Democratic . . . .
>
> So what's happened over the past six-plus months? Have we sub-30ers been so driven to prove Clinton's youth-shaming wrong that we've signed up by the millions with AmeriCorps and Teach for America?

> Most likely, Clinton's flip-flop on Generation Lazy has more to do with her and other presidential candidates' views on what constitutes proper and praiseworthy youth. To them (and many others in their age group), young folks are at their best when they perform tough work on the cheap or for free, and at their worst when they look for gratifying jobs that pay competitive salaries. Indeed, in that May speech in which Hillary **bemoaned** lazy youth, she decried the supposed "culture that has a premium on instant gratification," of which young people are supposedly a product.
>
> —Paul Thornton
> Campaign 2008, "In the Blogs"
> *Los Angeles Times*, November 5, 2007

36. beset

verb

To attack on all sides, to assail, to harass, as in *beset by financial difficulties*; to surround or hem in, as in *the little town beset on all sides with housing developments*; to place or set upon, as in *the ring beset with diamonds.*

Note: Often used as a verbal adjective.

> With such a goal in mind, the Iraqi government has budgeted more than $19 billion for public sector investment for 2008, but official spending is **beset** by corruption and sectarianism. U.S. military officers

> regularly complain that the education, health and water ministries bypass Sunni neighborhoods in west Baghdad.
>
> —Ned Parker
> "Iraq Calmer, But More Divided"
> *Los Angeles Times*, December 10, 2007

37. bilateral

adjective

Pertaining to two sides, parties, or factions, as in *a bilateral treaty*. In law, a *bilateral contract* binds two parties to reciprocal duties.

> Recently, President Bush and Iraqi Prime Minister Nouri al-Maliki signed a joint communiqué in which the U.S. committed to helping Iraq defend its government against internal and external threats. In response, the Maliki government asked for a one-year renewal of the current United Nation's Security Council Resolution that governs U.S. forces operating in Iraq. Mr. Maliki is also committed to working out **bilateral** relations with the U.S. to govern future American operations in his country.
>
> — Frederick W. Kagan
> "Our Friends in Baghdad"
> *Wall Street Journal*, December 21, 2007

38. blaspheme

verb

To speak irreverently of God or sacred things or beliefs; to speak evil of someone or something. Used as either a transitive verb (with object), as in *She blasphemed the pastor of her church*, or an intransitive verb (without object), as in *He blasphemed about all sacred things.*

Note: The related noun is *blasphemy.*

> Luis Buñuel pulled off a better trick 40 years ago, and with more economy, by posing Catherine Deneuve as St. Sebastian and flinging mud at her in "Belle de Jour." Though the reason Buñuel succeeded so brilliantly and enduringly is that he **blasphemed** a bigger modern god, that of celebrity.
>
> —Manohla Dargis
> Film Review of *Lunacy* (2005)
> *Los Angeles Times*, August 9, 2006

39. boorish

adjective

Like a boor, insensitive, crude; without good manners, as in *His boorish behavior offended everyone at the party.*

> Today's *New York Times* features a story on the **boorish** and disgusting behavior by large bunches of drunk and rowdy guys who hover around the ramps at Gate D at Giants Stadium and proceed to harass women to bare their breasts as well as throwing things at other fans, even kids.
>
> —Michael Sciannamea
> newyorkjets.com, November 20, 2007

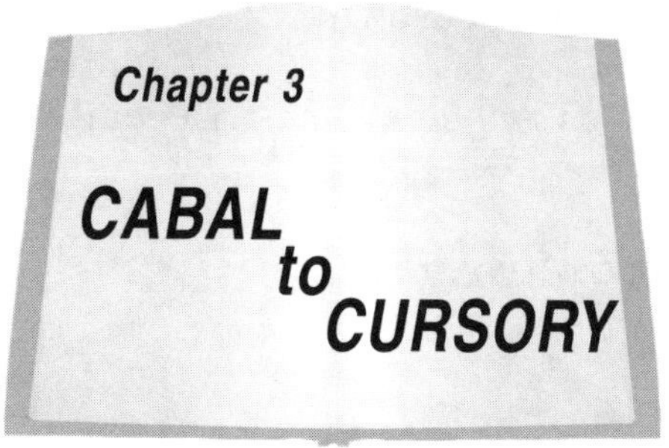

40. cabal

verb

To hatch a scheme, to plot.

noun

A small group of plotters who hatch a scheme against the government or persons in authority. The word also refers to the scheme itself.

> But now the British say Santa's corpulence isn't cute, it's a health hazard, an apple-shaped advertisement for Type 2 diabetes and heart disease. After a study released in October found that, by 2050, more than half of Britain's population will be obese, a **cabal** of fitness zealots at malls and shops in Merry Olde England decreed that their Santas must be trim. That's right—skinny Santas, buff Santas and, we tremble to think of it, Santas with six-pack abs. According to news reports, a shopping center in Kent even set up a boot camp for Santas who couldn't slim

down on their own.

—"Skinny Santas?"
Editorial, *Los Angeles Times*, December 24, 2007

41. cacophony

noun

A harsh and discordant sound; a meaningless mixture of sounds.

> Poets who know no better rhapsodize about the peace of nature, but a well-populated marsh is a **cacophony**.
>
> —Bern Keating
> "Birders' Heaven"
> *Connoisseur*, April 1986

42. calumny

noun

A false and misleading statement designed to destroy the reputation of someone or something; the act of uttering calumnies.

> It is harder to kill a whisper than even a shouted **calumny**.
>
> —Mary Stewart
> *The Last Enchantment* (1979)

43. cant

verb

To talk in a singsong, preaching, whining tone; to speak tediously with affected solemnity.

noun

Monotonous speech crammed with platitudes; the special vocabulary of a group or profession; whining speech.

> All gentle **cant** and philosophizing to the contrary notwithstanding, no people in this world ever did achieve their freedom by goody-goody talk and moral suasion: it being immutable law that all revolutions that will succeed, must begin in blood.
>
> —Mark Twain
> *A Connecticut Yankee in King Arthur's Court* (1889)

44. captious

adjective

One who finds fault, is difficult to please; designed to perplex or confuse, as in *captious questions.*

> Pat Oliphant's cartoon is notable because of the classic grace of the lines of the Statue of Liberty. The point is that freedom of speech has to be guaranteed to all, even a noisome fool like Mahmoud Ahmadinejad, if it is to be guaranteed to anyone. Thus the statue's inherent beauty has to be accurately drawn, to contrast with this **captious** little strutter.
>
> —Jeff Danziger
> "Classic Confusion"
> *Los Angeles Times*, September 30, 2007

45. caricature

noun

A picture or depiction that ludicrously exaggerates the features or defects of persons or things.

> The most perfect **caricature** is that which, on a small surface, with the simplest means, most accurately exaggerates, to the highest point, the peculiarities of a human being, at his most characteristic moment in the most beautiful manner.
>
> —Max Beerbohm
> "The Spirit of Caricature"
> *A Variety of Things* (1928)

46. castigate

verb

To criticize harshly; to punish for the purpose of correcting; to reprimand severely.

> How can you support a policy of racial preferences and then attack one of its supposed beneficiaries as undeserving? This, ultimately, is the intrinsic hypocrisy of the [Justice Clarence] Thomas bashers. They allege that he's not competent and that the only reason he became a Supreme Court justice was because he's black. And in so doing, they level the exact same arguments against Thomas that they **castigate** conservatives for making about affirmative action itself. But let's face facts: A program that gives people with a certain skin color

> an advantage will invariably reward some who would otherwise not qualify.
>
> —James Kirchick
> "Clarence Thomas Is Not the Hypocrite"
> *Los Angeles Times*, October 15, 2007

47. chagrin

verb

To vex by disappointment or humiliation, as in *The defeat chagrined him deeply.*

noun

A feeling of vexation; disappointment or humiliation.

> Silence is the universal refuge, the sequel to all dull discourses and all foolish acts, a balm to our every **chagrin**, as welcome after satiety as after disappointment; that background which the painter may not daub, be he master or bungler, and which, however awkward a figure we may have made in the foreground, remains ever our inviolable asylum, where no indignity can assail, no personality can disturb us.
>
> —Henry David Thoreau, "Friday"
> *A Week on the Concord and Merrimack Rivers* (1849)

48. charlatan

noun

A person pretending to have more knowledge or

skill than he or she actually possesses; a quack; a flamboyant deceiver.

> There is hardly any mental misery worse than that of having our own serious phrases, our own rooted beliefs, caricatured by a **charlatan** or a hireling.
>
> —George Eliot
> *Felix Holt* (1866)

49. circumlocution

noun

A roundabout way of speaking, usually using more words than necessary; evasion in speech or writing.

> Whatever was required to be done, the **Circumlocution** Office was beforehand with all the public departments in the art of perceiving How Not To Do It.
>
> —Charles Dickens
> *Little Dorrit* (1899)

50. circumscribe

verb

To draw a line around, to encircle, as in *to circumscribe a village on a map*; to enclose with bounds, to delimit, as in *His ambition is circumscribed by his lack of drive and determination.*

> [U]ntil women assume the place in society which good sense and good feeling alike assign to them, human improvement must advance but feebly. It is in vain that we would

circumscribe the power of one half of our race, and that half by far the most important and influential.

—Frances Wright
Quoted in *Feminism: The Essential Historical Writings* by Miriam Schnier (1972)

51. circumspect

adjective

Watchful, discreet, cautious, prudent, as in *a circumspect investment strategy.*

I smiled,
I waited,
I was **circumspect**;
O never, never, never write that I
missed life or loving.

—Hilda Doolittle
"A Dead Priestess Speaks"

52. cogent

adjective

Incisive, analytical, convincing, believable because of a forcible and clear presentation.

[C]ider-apples furnish one of the most **cogent** arguments to prove that Providence had the production of alcoholic liquors directly in its eye.

—George Saintsbury
"Beer and Cider"
Modern Essays (1921)

53. cognizant

adjective

Fully informed, aware, conscious.

Note: Usually followed by the preposition *of*, as in *He was cognizant of the dangers.*

> In my own view, there are clear differences between child and adult artistic activity. While the child may be aware that he is doing things differently from others, he does not fully appreciate the rules and conventions of symbolic realms; his adventurousness holds little significance. In contrast, the adult artist is fully **cognizant** of the norms embraced by others; his willingness, his compulsion, to reject convention is purchased, at the very least, with full knowledge of what he is doing and often at considerable psychic cost to himself. As Picasso once remarked, "I used to draw like Raphael, but it has taken me a whole lifetime to learn to draw like a child."
>
> —Howard Gardner
> *Art, Mind, and Brain: A Cognitive Approach to Creativity* (1982)

54. colloquialism, colloquial

noun

Colloquialism: an ordinary or familiar expression; familiar style or usage.

adjective

Colloquial: appropriate to or characteristic of ordinary or familiar conversation instead of formal speech or writing.

> **Colloquial** poetry is to the real art as the barber's wax dummy is to sculpture.
>
> —Ezra Pound
> "I Gather the Limbs of Osiris"
> *Selected Prose* 1909–1965 (1973)

55. complement, compliment

verb

Complement: to complete, to add to something, to provide something felt to be lacking, as in *The two books complemented each other and provided a complete picture of the war.*

Compliment: to praise or extol, as in *She complimented him on his performance.*

noun

Complement: something that completes or makes perfect, as in *The fine red wine was the perfect complement to the aged steak.*

Compliment: an expression of praise or admiration, as in *Her boss's compliment raised her spirits.*

56. comport

verb

To conduct or behave (oneself), as in *He comported himself with dignity*; to be in agreement with (usually followed by *with*), as in *Our policy must comport with the principles of free enterprise.*

> Christians, like 12-step group attendees, are people who are committed to becoming, to use the Apostle Paul's phrase, new creatures. Living sexual lives that **comport** with the Gospel is one part of that. Perhaps pledges for chastity need to be made not only by the individual teenager. Perhaps we also need pledges made by the teenager's whole Christian community: we pledge to support you in this difficult, countercultural choice; we pledge that the church is a place where you can lay bare your brokenness and sin, where you don't have to dissemble; we pledge to cheer you on when chastity seems unbearably difficult, and we pledge to speak God's forgiveness to you if you falter. No retooled pledge will guarantee teenagers' chastity, but words of grace and communal commitment are perhaps a firmer basis for sexual ethics than simple assertions that true love waits.
>
> —Lauren F. Winner
> "Saving Grace"
> *New York Times*, May 19, 2006

57. compunction

noun

A feeling of anxiety or discomfort caused by regret for doing wrong or causing pain; contrition; remorse; any uneasiness or hesitation about the rightness of an action.

> Torture, presented with gusto and almost no moral **compunction**, is an increasingly popular way of gathering intelligence on [the TV show] *24*. If anything, the new season seems even more intent on hammering home the message that torture is necessary in the war against terror, and that despite what some experts claim, torture works.
>
> —Alessandra Stanley
> "Suicide Bombers Strike,
> and America Is in Turmoil. It's Just
> Another Day in the Life of Jack Bauer"
> *New York Times*, January 12, 2007

58. comprise

verb

To include, contain, consist of.

Note: Correct, and traditional usage, requires the use of *comprise* in a way whereby the whole *comprises* the parts, as in *The United States comprises 50 states.* Increasingly, writers use the verb in a passive-voice construction: *to be comprised of,* as in *The United States is comprised of 50 states.*

Consider the following usage note from Dictionary.com:

> *Comprise* has had an interesting history of sense development. In addition to its original

senses, dating from the 15th century, "to include" and "to consist of" (*The United States of America comprises 50 states*), *comprise* has had since the late 18th century the meaning "to form or constitute" (*Fifty states comprise the United States of America*). Since the late 19th century it has also been used in passive constructions with a sense synonymous with that of one of its original meanings "to consist of, be composed of": *The United States of America is comprised of 50 states.* These later uses are often criticized, but they occur with increasing frequency even in formal speech and writing.

—Dictionary.reference.com/ browse/comprise

59. condescend

verb

Three meanings:

1. To behave as if conscious of descending from a superior position, rank, or dignity, as in *The wealthy art patron, seemingly put upon, condescended to attend the "new art" exhibit.*

2. To stoop to do something, as in *He would not condescend to misrepresent the situation.*

3. To voluntarily assume equality with one regarded as inferior, as in *He condescended to their level of knowledge in order to be understood.*

60. connote

verb

To suggest or signify something in addition to the primary meaning, as in *A hot cup of tea connotes hospitality and comfort.*

> With so many mass-market goods made offshore, American-made products, which are often more expensive, have come to **connote** luxury.
>
> —Alex Williams
> "Love It? Check the Label"
> *New York Times*, September 6, 2007

Note: *Denote* and *connote* are often confused because both words have senses that entail signification. *Denote* means "to signify directly or literally" and describes the relation between the word and the thing it conventionally names.

> *Connote* means "to signify indirectly, suggest or imply" and describes the relation between the word and the images or associations it evokes. Thus, the word *river* denotes a moving body of water and may *connote* such things as the relentlessness of time and the changing nature of life.
> —Dictionary.reference.com/browse/denote

61. consummate

verb

To bring to completion, to fulfill; to complete an arrangement or an undertaking, as in *to consummate the deal*; to complete a marital union through sexual intercourse.

adjective

Highly skilled, superb, as in *a consummate musician*; of the highest degree, as in *an act of consummate loyalty.*

> Here was the **consummate** "good German" who dared criticize Hitler's racist policies to his face. But on another occasion, late in the war, she held her tongue and was "nearly sick" after returning in 1938 to Nazi Germany and discovering the horrors of Kristallnacht, the nationwide pogrom of German Jews the year before Hitler began World War II.
>
> —Halton Adler Mann
> Letter to the Editor
> *Washington Post*, April 3, 1994

62. contemptible, contemptuous

adjective

Contemptible: Worthy of scorn or disdain, despicable.

Contemptuous: Showing or expressing contempt or disdain.

Note: One would be *contemptuous* of a *contemptible* act.

> The story unfolds as Liberti's diary, an account by turns despairing, courageous,

rawly sexual, bewildered and philosophical—at times wearily **contemptuous** of his comrades, at times movingly affectionate. It is, in other words, a convincing portrait of a small combat unit under great stress. It's also a compelling window on contemporary young Israel. Part of what engages the reader is the opportunity to learn the soldiers' slang and feel their struggle to subdue emotional experiences no young man should have to bear, like the loss of comrades.

—Tim Ruttan
Book Review of *Beaufort: A Novel*
by Ron Leshem
Los Angeles Times, December 26, 2007

63. continual, continuous

adjective

Continual: regular or frequent events or occurrences, as in *continual trips to the doctor.* A good synonym is *intermittent.*

Continuous: uninterrupted in time or space, as in *continuous talking by the people behind you at the movie.* A good synonym is *uninterrupted.*

Note: Most usage guides stress the differences between *continual* and *continuous*, but accomplished writers have ignored the distinctions. Consequently, if you need to show that something is *continual*, use *intermittent.* If you need to show that something is *continuous*, use *uninterrupted.* However, a hard distinction remains for spatial relationships, as in *a continuous series of doorways*, not *a continual series of doorways.*

64. contravene

verb

To conflict with, to go against, to deny or oppose, as in *He contravened his opponent's position with an array of data*; to violate or transgress, as in *She contravened the election laws.*

> The *Times* also detailed an investment of $3.3 billion in one of the Sudan-linked firms by Berkshire Hathaway Inc., whose chief executive, Warren E. Buffett, has pledged $31 billion of his personal fortune, held in Berkshire stock, to the Gates Foundation. These investments by the foundation and by Berkshire **contravened** the foundation's donations to groups providing relief for Darfur refugees.
>
> —Charles Piller
> "Foundations Align Investments with Their Charitable Goals"
> *Los Angeles Times*, December 29, 2007

65. corollary

noun

A proposition following so obviously from another that it requires little demonstration.

> The **corollary** to Cheney's zealous embrace of secrecy is his near total aversion to the notion of accountability. I've never seen a former member of the House of Representatives demonstrate such contempt for Congress—even when it was controlled by his own party.

—Walter F. Mondale
"Answering to No One"
Washington Post, July 29, 2007

66. correlate, correlative, correlation

verb

Correlate: to establish an orderly connection or relation; to have, or stand in, a relation.
adjective

adjective

Correlative: mutually or reciprocally related.noun

noun

Correlation: either one of two related things, especially when one implies the other.

> But what about IQ? Aren't today's rich more likely to have higher IQs than the general population?
>
> Apparently not. At least not according to a new study by Jay Zagorsky, a research scientist at the Ohio State University's Center for Human Resource Research, which found that the wealthy aren't more likely to have higher IQs than the general population. . . . In combing the data, Mr. Zagorsky found no meaningful **correlation** between large wealth and high IQ scores.
>
> —Robert Frank, "You Don't Have to Be Smart to Be Rich"
> *Wall Street Journal*, May 1, 2007

67. corroboration, corroborate

noun

Corroboration: the act of making more certain, the act of *corroborating.*

verb

Corroborate: to make more certain, to confirm; to strengthen or support with other evidence.

> A newly released video that was obtained by Britain's Channel 4 and broadcast Monday cast doubt on the government's claims and appeared to **corroborate** witnesses' stories. The footage appeared to show a gunman and a suspected suicide bomber approaching Bhutto's sport-utility vehicle. Seconds later, the video showed gunfire and Bhutto's hair and scarf being blown back just as a bomb explodes.
>
> —Emily Wax and Griff Witte
> "Doctors Cite Pressure to Keep Silent on Bhutto"
> *Washington Post*, January 1, 2008

68. credence

noun

Acceptance as true or valid; belief.

> A letter found in 1991 by State Archivist David Olson lends **credence** to another more direct theory [on the origin of "Tar Heels"]. A letter from Maj. Joseph Engelhard describes a fight involving men from North Carolina

> in which Lee was heard to have said, "There they stand as if they have tar on their heels."
>
> —tarheelblue.cstv.com/trads/unc-trads-whytar.html

69. credible, credulous

adjective

Credible: capable of being believed; worthy of belief, as in *a credible witness*.
Credulous: willing to believe too readily; gullible.

Note: The term *incredulous* means disinclined to believe, skeptical.

> Today's preferred methods haven't changed much since political polling's nadir, in 1948, when erroneous pre-election surveys were relied on by the **credulous** press to predict a victory for Republican Thomas Dewey over Harry Truman. In one of its editions printed on election night, the Chicago Daily Tribune ran the infamous headline, "Dewey Defeats Truman."
>
> —Carl Bialik
> "Grading the Pollsters"
> *Wall Street Journal*, November 16, 2006

70. criterion

noun

A standard, rule, or principle by which to determine the correctness of a judgment or conclusion.

Note: The word *criterion* is singular. Though *criterions* is an acceptable plural form, most usage panels and writers use *criteria* as the plural. The plural *criteria*, which often appears in the singular in speech, should never be used as a singular in proper writing.

> Up to 25 percent of people in whom psychiatrists would currently diagnose depression may only be reacting normally to stressful events such as a divorce or losing a job, according to a new analysis that reexamined how the standard diagnostic **criteria** are used.
>
> —Shankar Vedantam
> "Criteria for Depression Are Too Broad, Researchers Say"
> *Washington Post*, April 3, 2007

71. culpable

adjective

Guilty, deserving blame or censure, blameworthy.

> "You were a full participant, and you were at least equally **culpable** with every other man sentenced in this case," Hudson told Vick.
>
> —U.S. District Judge Henry E. Hudson
> sentencing Michael Vick on charges
> of illegal dog fighting, December 11, 2007

72. cursory

adjective

Rapid and superficial, hasty without noticing details, not thorough.

"In India, there is the priestly caste . . . ," "The Arunta, an aboriginal tribe from central Australia . . . ," "In the tongue of the Piscataway Indians who first occupied Potomac Land. . . ." Of course, these **cursory** cultural excursions are merely tongue-in-cheek set-ups for the Potomac Land institutions that follow: the curious rituals (face time), rites of solidarity (fundraisers), fictive kinship (party affiliation), Kabuki theater (judicial confirmation hearings), purification rituals (the Gridiron Club) and shadow puppets (pundits), to name only a few.

—Robert Leopold
Book Review of *Homo Politicus* by Dana Milbank
Washington Post, January 6, 2008

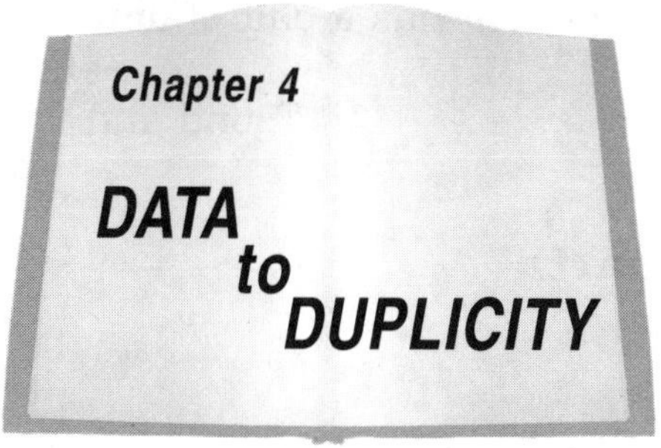

73. data, datum

noun

Facts, statistics, or items of information.

Note: *Data* is a plural of *datum*, which is originally a Latin noun meaning "something given." Today, *data* is used in English both as a plural noun meaning "facts or pieces of information" (*These data are described more fully elsewhere*) and as a singular mass noun meaning "information": *Not much data is available on flood control in Brazil.* It is almost always treated as a plural in scientific and academic writing. In other types of writing it is either singular or plural. The singular *datum* meaning "a piece of information" is now rare in all types of writing. In surveying and civil engineering, where *datum* has specialized senses, the plural form is *datums.*

—Dictionary.reference.com/browse/data

74. dauntless

adjective

Fearless, intrepid, bold.

> For Thought has a pair of **dauntless** wings.
>
> —Robert Frost
> "Bond and Free" (1920)

75. dearth

noun

Scarcity, inadequate supply (usually of something desirable).

> Reverence is the highest quality of man's nature; and that individual, or nation, which has it slightly developed, is so far unfortunate. It is a strong spiritual instinct, and seeks to form channels for itself where none exists; thus Americans, in the **dearth** of other objects to worship, fall to worshipping themselves.
>
> —Lydia M. Child
> *Letters from New York* (1843)

76. debase

verb

To lower in character or virtue, to reduce in value or quality, as in *The Fed debased the dollar*; to lower in rank, significance, or dignity.

> Hygiene is the corruption of medicine by morality. It is impossible to find a hygienest who does not **debase** his theory of the healthful with a theory of the virtuous.... The true aim of medicine is not to make men

virtuous; it is to safeguard and rescue them from the consequences of their vices.

—H. L. Mencken
"The Physician"
Prejudices (1922)

77. decimate

verb

To destroy a measurable or large proportion of.

Note: Originally, *decimate* meant to select by lot and execute every tenth soldier of a unit. But the current usage of the word, originating in the 19th century, means to destroy a large amount of something. But because of the "one-tenth" sense of the word, careful writers avoid accompanying *decimate* with percentages, as in *Bird flu decimated 80% of the flock.* Instead, use *destroyed.*

The rain forests continue to be **decimated**.

— "The American Environmental Movement, A Master Plan for Political Victory"
worldfuturefund.org/wffmaster/Reports/wff-es.html

78. decorous

adjective

Characterized by dignity, good manners, good taste, appropriateness.

Note: *Decorum* is the noun form.

> But, by a curious twist, it is not the leadership that is old and **decorous** that fetches him [the American], but the leadership that is new and extravagant. He will resist dictation out of the past, but he will follow a new messiah with almost Russian willingness, and into the wildest vagaries of economics, religion, morals and speech. A new fallacy in politics spreads faster in the United States than anywhere else on earth, and so does a new fashion in hats, or a new revelation of God, or a new means of killing time, or a new shibboleth, or metaphor, or piece of slang.
>
> —H. L. Mencken
> *The American Language* (1921)

79. deduce

verb

To derive or draw as a conclusion by reasoning from given premises or principles.

> In no department are American universities weaker than in the department of English. The æsthetic opinion that they disseminate is flabby and childish, and their philological work in the national language is extraordinarily lacking in enterprise. No attempt to **deduce** the principles of vulgar American grammar from the everyday speech of the people has ever been made by an American philologist.
>
> —H. L. Mencken
> *The American Language* (1921)

80. degradation

noun

Diminution, as of strength or magnitude; changing to a lower or less respected state.

Note: *Degrade* is the verb form.

> [Former U.S. Sen. David Boren] went on to say that the country's standing in the world has sunk to unprecedented lows and problems such as budget deficits, energy supply and environmental **degradation** are not being addressed.
>
> —Jeff Franks
> "Bloomberg, Moderates Lament State of U.S."
> *Reuters*, January 7, 2008

81. deign

verb

To deem worthy of notice or account; to think it appropriate to one's dignity.

> No professor, so far as I know, has ever **deigned** to give the same sober attention to the *sermo plebeius* [uneducated speech] of his country that his colleagues habitually give to the pronunciation of Latin, or to the irregular verbs in French.
>
> —H. L. Mencken
> *The American Language* (1921)

82. deleterious

adjective

Harmful or injurious, morally or physically.

> I will follow that system of regimen which, according to my ability and judgment, I consider for the benefit of my patients, and abstain from whatever is **deleterious** and mischievous. I will give no deadly medicine to any one if asked, nor suggest any such counsel; and in like manner I will not give to a woman a pessary to produce abortion.
>
> —Hippocrates
>
> The Oath and Law of Hippocrates

83. delineate

verb

To represent by sketch or diagram; to trace the outline of; sketch or trace in outline; to represent pictorially, as in *She delineated the state of New York on the map with a blue pencil.* To portray in words; describe or outline with precision, as in *He delineated the annual budget to the audience.*

> But I shall endeavour in this Discourse to describe the paths I have followed, and to **delineate** my life as in a picture, in order that each one may be able to judge of them for himself, and that in the general opinion entertained of them, as gathered from current report, I myself may have a new help

towards instruction to be added to those I have been in the habit of employing.

—René Descartes
Discourse on Method (1637)

84. demagogue

noun

An orator or politician who gains popularity and power by arousing emotions, passions, and prejudices.

> We shall achieve industrial democracy because we shall steer a similar middle course between the extreme individualist and the Socialist, between the **demagogue** who attacks all wealth and who can see no wrong done anywhere unless it is perpetrated by a man of wealth, and the apologist for the plutocracy who rails against so much as a restatement of the eighth commandment [against stealing] upon the ground that it will "hurt business."
>
> —Theodore Roosevelt
> *History as Literature* (1913)

85. demonstrable, demonstrative

adjective

Demonstrable: capable of being demonstrated by positive proof; clearly evident or obvious.

> It is plain and **demonstrable**, that much ale is not good for a Yankee, and operates

> differently upon them from what it does upon a Briton; ale must be drank in a fog and a drizzle.
>
> —Herman Melville
> *The Writings of Herman Melville* (1969)

Demonstrative: characterized or given to open expression of one's emotions or attitudes.

Note: In grammar, a *demonstrative pronoun* or *demonstrative adjective* (*this, that, these, those*) indicates or singles out the thing referred to.

> Whenever you pray, make sure you do it at school assemblies and football games, like the **demonstrative** creatures who pray before large television audiences. That is the real goal of the thing. But do not, I urge you, pray all alone in your home where no one can see. That does not get you ratings.
>
> —Garry Wills
> Author of the Pulitzer Prize-winning
> *Lincoln at Gettysburg*
> Quoted in *Baltimore Sun*, November 22, 1994

86. denizen

noun

Inhabitant or resident; one who frequently inhabits a place, as in *the denizens of the local pub.*

> A tanned skin is something more than respectable, and perhaps olive is a fitter color than white for a man,—a **denizen** of the

woods. "The pale white man!" I do not wonder that the African pitied him.

—Henry David Thoreau
"Walking" (1862)
The Writings of Henry David Thoreau (1906)

87. denote

verb

To indicate, to be a sign of, as in *A rise in the price of gold often denotes a fall in the U.S. dollar.*

Note: *Denote* and *connote* are often confused because both words have senses that entail signification. *Denote* means "to signify directly or literally" and describes the relation between the word and the thing it conventionally names. *Connote* means "to signify indirectly, suggest or imply" and describes the relation between the word and the images or associations it evokes. Thus, the word *river* denotes a moving body of water and may *connote* such things as the relentlessness of time and the changing nature of life.

—Dictionary.reference.com/browse/denote

88. denouement

noun

The final resolution of a plot or play; also used to describe the ultimate outcome of a doubtful series of events.

A young professor I watched in action at one of our large eastern colleges used to stand with his back to the class and mumble explanations of blackboard problems. He was "let out" at the end of two years because students refused to attend his classes. He was given an evasive reason for his dismissal and he left with justifiable bitterness toward the administration. If someone had told him the truth he could have avoided this **denouement**. Sometimes professors go on for years without any conception of remediable faults which irritate their listeners.

—Mary Barnett Gilson
What's Past Is Prologue (1940)

89. deprecate

verb
To express disapproval of; to belittle.

One of the running gags in "Looking for Comedy in the Muslim World" is that Albert Brooks—the director, screenwriter and star, as well as the main character—is best known around the world for his role in "Finding Nemo." Or as it is more frequently and humiliatingly put, for playing a talking fish in a cartoon.

Mr. Brooks likes to **deprecate** both himself and the work for hire he does in Hollywood, but the difference between "Nemo" and his own films may not be as great as he pretends.

—A. O. Scott
"Looking for Comedy in the Muslim World"
New York Times, January 20, 2006

90. despot, despotism

noun

Despot: a monarch or other ruler with absolute power; a tyrant or oppressor.

Despotism: rule by an autocratic government; tyranny; a country ruled by a despot.

> There are three kinds of **despots**. There is the **despot** who tyrannises over the body. There is the **despot** who tyrannises over the soul. There is the **despot** who tyrannises over the soul and body alike. The first is called the Prince. The second is called the Pope. The third is called the People.
>
> —Oscar Wilde
> "The Soul of Man Under Socialism"
> *Fortnightly Review*, February 1891

91. didactic

adjective

Pertaining to teaching, intended for instruction; inclined to teach or lecture (to excess), as in *a boring, didactic speaker.*

> A **didactic** play attempts to explain what man must do to make the world better and life more rational; a tragedy shows that life will never be rational and the world will never be good. Long before Bertolt Brecht, German culture was enamored with parables about the triumph of reason. Yet man is a tragic being, irrational and divided within himself,

> and so it is an enthralling spectacle when a life charted as a **didactic** play unexpectedly reveals a tragic aspect.
>
> —Daniel Kehlmann
> "A Prisoner of the Nobel"
> *New York Times*, August 20, 2006

92. diffident

adjective

Lacking confidence in one's own ability or worth; timid, shy.

> [Treasury Secretary Nicholas F. Brady] is bland on television and awkward as a public speaker. In a city of bombast and pomposity, Mr. Brady is unusually gentle and modest, a man who can and often does enter a restaurant or a large party unrecognized. At international meetings, he has taken pains not to stand out from the ministers of other countries. . . .
>
> "In all my years in Washington," said an admirer who has served here in several different capacities in the Government over the last 35 years, "I don't recall a Treasury Secretary as **diffident** as Brady."
>
> —David E. Rosenbaum
> "The Treasury's 'Mr. Diffident'"
> *New York Times*, November 19, 1989

93. dilatory

adjective

Tending to delay or procrastinate; tardy, slow.

> Diligence increaseth the fruit of toil. A **dilatory** man wrestles with losses.
>
> —Hesiod
> *Works and Days*

94. dilettante

noun

One who engages in art or other subject for amusement, usually in a desultory or superficial way; a dabbler. Also used to refer to a lover of the fine arts.

> The second reason for his delay was a personal one. He had dawdled over his cigar because he was at heart a **dilettante**, and thinking over a pleasure to come often gave him a subtler satisfaction than its realisation.
>
> —Edith Wharton
> *The Age of Innocence* (1920)

95. diminution

noun

The process, act, or fact of lessening or diminishing; reduction.

Note: The adjective form *diminutive* often refers to people or things that are small or short. In grammar, a *diminutive* formation denotes smallness, familiarity, or triviality; the suffix *-let* in *droplet* produces a *diminutive* element.

> Every **diminution** of the public burdens arising from taxation gives to individual enterprise increased power and furnishes to all the members of our happy confederacy new motives for patriotic affection and support.
>
> —President Andrew Jackson
> Sixth Annual Message to Congress,
> December 1, 1834

96. discomfit

verb

Discomfit, to confuse, disconcert; to thwart, to frustrate the plans of, to foil.

> Whether the issue is birth control or global warming or clean air, this administration has already acquired a special place in regulatory history for the audacity with which it has manipulated or muzzled science (and in some cases individual scientists) that might **discomfit** its industrial allies or interfere with its political agenda.
>
> — Editorial
> "Muzzling Those Pesky Scientists"
> *New York Times*, December 11, 2006

97. disenfranchise

verb

To deprive of any right privilege or power; to deprive of voting rights.

> From the early indications, Americans are

> feeling enthusiastic about their constitutionally guaranteed right to vote. The Supreme Court should encourage, not frustrate, that enthusiasm when it hears a challenge today to a harsh voter identification law adopted by Indiana. The law aims to be an anti-fraud measure, but its main impact will be to **disenfranchise** large numbers of registered voters. The court should not let it stand.
>
> —Editorial
> *New York Times*, January 9, 2008

98. disingenuous

See the discussion of *ingenuous*.

99. disjunctive

adjective

Helping or serving to disconnect or separate; dividing; distinguishing.

Note: In grammar, *disjunctive* describes the process of syntactically setting two or more elements in opposition to each other, as in *poor* ***but*** *happy*, or expressing an alternative, as in *John* ***or*** *Mary*. A *disjunctive* series of elements is joined by the coordinating conjunction *or*, and any one element of the series may satisfy the proposition.

> The Federal Rules of Criminal Procedure phrase the sanction provision somewhat differently, but retain the **disjunctive** form: "[T]he court *shall order* that the testimony of the witness be stricken from the record

> and that the trial proceed, **or** . . . *shall declare* a mistrial if required by the interest of justice." Fed. R. Crim. P. 26.2(e).
>
> The government seizes upon the **disjunctive** form of this language to argue that a district court may never impose both the sanction of a mistrial and the sanction of suppressing the testimony of the witness when a Jencks Act violation occurs.
>
> —*United States v. McKoy*
> U.S. Court of Appeals for the Ninth Circuit,
> March 4, 1996

100. disparage

verb

To regard or speak of slightingly; to belittle; to bring reproach or discredit on.

> People **disparage** knowing and the intellectual life, and urge doing. I am content with knowing, if only I could know.
>
> —Ralph Waldo Emerson
> "Experience"
> *Essays* (1844)

101. dissemble

verb

To give a misleading or false appearance, to conceal the truth; to feign.

Note: Do not confuse *dissemble* (to hide the truth) with *disassemble* (to take something apart).

Consider this note from Washington State University's website:

> People who **dissemble** are being dishonest, trying to hide what they are really up to. This is an uncommon word, often misused when "disassemble" is meant. People who disassemble something take it apart—they are doing the opposite of assembling it.
>
> — www.wsu.edu/~brians/errors/**dissemble**.html

102. disseminate

verb

To spread or scatter widely, as seed is sown; to distribute, broadcast, disperse, as in *disseminate information.*

> Nations, like individuals, wish to enjoy a fair reputation. It is therefore desirable for us that the slanders on our country, **disseminated** by hired or prejudiced travellers, should be corrected.
>
> —Thomas Jefferson to James Ogilvie, 1811 etext.lib.virginia.edu/jefferson/quotations/jeff1600.htm

103. dogma, dogmatic, dogmatize

noun

Dogma: a systems of tenets or principles, often from a church; prescribed doctrine, as in *political dogma*; a settled or established belief or opinion.

adjective

Dogmatic: often used to describe a person who rigidly adheres to a belief or who tries to convert others to that belief.

verb

Dogmatize: to express one's firm set of beliefs.

> We think that if we simply call someone conservative, anti-choice and anti-civil rights, that's enough to scare people to our side. But that tired **dogma** won't hunt in today's electorate, which is far more independent-thinking and complex in its views on values than our side presumes.
>
> —Dan Gerstein
> "Base Dogma"
> *Wall Street Journal*, January 22, 2006

104. duplicity

noun

Deceitfulness in conduct or speech; speaking and acting in two different, opposing ways; a twofold or double quality or state.

Note: The adjective *duplicitous* describes someone who is given to deceitful conduct or speech; a person who is two-faced.

> Since North Korea's inception as a totalitarian state in 1948, Pyongyang has

had only two rulers—Kim Il Sung (installed by Stalin) and his son, Kim Jong Il, who took charge after his father's death in 1994. The junior Kim's record over the past dozen years is not one of reform, but of brutality, **duplicity** and blackmail.

—Claudia Rosett
"Food for Nukes?"
Wall Street Journal, February 19, 2006

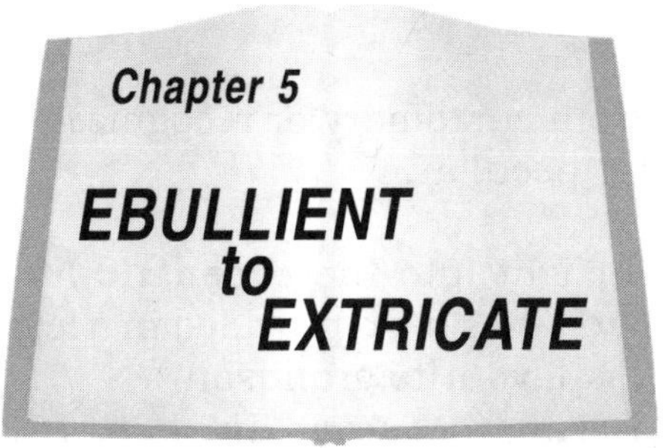

105. ebullient

adjective

Showing enthusiasm or exhilaration of feeling; excited; high-spirited.

> The world was kept informed of Pavarotti's *joie de vivre*, his **ebullient** flirtations and his halfhearted struggle with his weight, which fluctuated between 250 and 350 pounds. At the peak of his career, he received more than 50,000 fan letters a year, and it was said that he never turned down a request for an autograph, a picture or a kiss.
>
> —Tim Page
> "Opera World Loses a Leading Ambassador"
> *Washington Post*, September 6, 2007

106. eccentric

noun

One who goes his own way and cares little about the norm.

adjective

Deviating from customary or recognized character; erratic; odd; peculiar.

> An insight into the **eccentric** life of Albert Einstein has been provided in a letter written by his favourite grandson.
>
> Bernhard Caesar Einstein, 75, who has never previously spoken about his relative, has recounted a string of anecdotes about the often bizarre life of the 20th century's greatest scientist.
>
> At one point, the younger Mr. Einstein recalled, his grandfather resorted to collecting cigarette butts from the streets to circumvent his doctor's effort to stop him from smoking.
>
> —Justin Stares
> "Einstein, **Eccentric** Genius, Smoked Butts Picked Up Off Street"
> *The Telegraph*, May 11, 2005

107. efface

verb

To wipe out, do away with, obliterate, expunge, as in *She effaced her most dreadful memories.*

Note: The related terms *self-effacement* and *self-effacing* mean to keep oneself in the background, to exhibit humility.

> If we work upon marble, it will perish; if we work on brass, time will **efface** it. If we rear temples, they will crumble to dust. But if we

> work on men's immortal minds, if we impress on them high principles, the just fear of God, and love for their fellow-men, we engrave on those tablets something which no time can **efface**, and which will brighten and brighten to all eternity.
>
> —Former Secretary of State Daniel Webster
> Speech to the City Council of Boston, Massachusetts, May 22, 1852
> *The Writings and Speeches of Daniel Webster* (1903)

108. effete

adjective

Lacking in wholesome vigor, degenerate, decadent; exhausted of energy or support, worn out.

> A spirit of national masochism prevails, encouraged by an **effete** corps of impudent snobs who characterize themselves as intellectuals.
>
> —Former Vice President Spiro T. Agnew
> Speech at a Republican Fund-Raising Dinner, New Orleans, Louisiana, October 19, 1969
> *Collected Speeches of Spiro Agnew* (1971)

109. efficacious

adjective

Capable of having the desired result; effective as a method, means, or remedy.

Note: The noun form *efficacy* means effectiveness. For example, to gain FDA approval, a drug company must show the *efficacy* of the drug.

> The **efficacy** of religion lies precisely in what is not rational, philosophic or eternal; its **efficacy** lies in the unforeseen, the miraculous, the extraordinary.
>
> —Henri Frédéric Amiel
> *Journal* (1885)

110. effrontery

noun

Unblushing impudence or boldness; barefaced audacity; "nerve."

Note: Do not confuse the noun *effrontery* with the verb and noun *affront.*

> The verb *affront* means "to insult, to offend deliberately"; the noun means "insult" and takes *to* or, less frequently, *of: I couldn't forgive his affront to* [*of*] *his mother. Effrontery* is "impudence, boldness, audacity, presumption": *She then had the effrontery to ask a favor.*
>
> —Kenneth G. Wilson
> *The Columbia Guide to Standard American English* (1993)

111. egoism, egotism

noun

Egoism: a philosophical doctrine that morality has its foundations in self-interest.

Egotism: an excessive preoccupation with self.

Note: *Egotism, egoism* refer to preoccupation with one's ego or self. *Egotism* is the common word for obtrusive and excessive reference to and emphasis upon oneself and one's own importance: *His egotism alienated all his friends. Egoism*, a less common word, is used especially in philosophy, ethics, or metaphysics, where it emphasizes the importance of or preoccupation with self in relation to other things: *sufficient egoism to understand one's central place in the universe.*

—dictionary.reference.com/
browse/egotism

112. egregious

adjective

Extraordinary in a bad way, glaring, flagrant, as in *an egregious violation of the law.*

> On Jan. 31, 1996, the city ordered the tenants of a Harlem brownstone to move out, saying that a series of code violations had made the building too hazardous to be occupied. . . . "These are **egregious** code violations," Carol Abrams, a spokeswoman for the City Department of Housing Preservation and Development, said yesterday.
>
> —Terry Pristin
> "Building Owned by Charity
> Had '**Egregious**' Violations"
> *New York Times*, April 19, 2001

113. elicit, illicit

verb

Elicit: to draw out, to bring forth, to call forth or provoke.

Illicit: not legally permitted or authorized, disapproved of, as in *an illicit affair* or *illicit drug traffic.*

> It is the story-teller's task to **elicit** sympathy and a measure of understanding for those who lie outside the boundaries of State approval.
>
> —Graham Greene
> Speech on receiving the Shakespeare Prize, awarded by the University of Hamburg, Germany, 1969

114. elucidate

verb

To bring out more clearly the facts concerning; to make lucid or clear.

> The chief element in the art of statesmanship under modern conditions is the ability to **elucidate** the confused and clamorous interests which converge upon the seat of government. It is an ability to penetrate from the naïve self-interest of each group to its permanent and real interest. . . . Statesmanship . . . consists in giving the

> people not what they want but what they will learn to want.
>
> —Walter Lippmann
> *A Preface to Morals* (1929)

115. elude, allude

verb

Elude: to evade the search or pursuit of by dexterity or artifice; to escape capture. Also, to escape the understanding of, as in *The answer eluded me.*

Allude: to refer to casually or indirectly.

> If you want something, it will **elude** you. If you do not want something, you will get ten of it in the mail.
>
> —*New York Times*
> Anna Quindlen
> *Living Out Loud* (1988)

116. emaciate

verb

To waste away in flesh, to make abnormally lean. Often used as a verbal adjective, as in *After his diet, he looked emaciated.*

> It never entered his head to analyse the details of the sick man's situation, to consider how that body was lying under the quilt, how those **emaciated** legs and thighs and spine were lying huddled up, and whether they could not be made more

> comfortable, whether anything could not be done to make things, if not better, at least less bad. It made his blood run cold when he began to think of all these details.
>
> —Leo Tolstoy
> *Anna Karenin* (1877)

117. emanate

verb

To flow out of, to proceed, as from a source, as in *The light emanated from the lamp.*

> As the struggle proceeded for making the ruling power **emanate** from the periodical choice of the ruled, some persons began to think that too much importance had been attached to the limitation of the power itself. *That* (it might seem) was a resource against rulers whose interests were habitually opposed to those of the people. What was now wanted was, that the rulers should be identified with the people; that their interest and will should be the interest and will of the nation. The nation did not need to be protected against its own will.
>
> —John Stuart Mill
> *On Liberty* (1863)

118. emigrate, immigrate

verb

Emigrate: to move out of a country.

Immigrate: to come into a country.

noun

Emigration: the process of leaving a country.
Emigrant: the person who leaves.

Immigration: process of coming into a country.
Immigrant: the person who comes in.

Note: Use this trick. ***E****migrate* = ***e****xit*; ***i****mmigrate* = come ***in***.

> One of the most important issues in this year's presidential campaign is an issue that most leading contenders have been reluctant to discuss in a serious way: illegal **immigration**.
>
> —Editorial "The Candidates and Illegal Immigration" *Washington Times*, January 2, 2008

119. eminent, imminent

adjective

Eminent: high in station or rank, prominent, distinguished; conspicuous. To show the highest in stature, use *preeminent* (no hyphen).
In law, the power of *eminent domain* is the power of a government to take private property for public use.

> With the single exception of Homer, there is no **eminent** writer, not even Sir Walter Scott, whom I can despise so entirely as I despise Shakespear when I measure my mind against his.... But I am bound to add that I

> pity the man who cannot enjoy Shakespear. He has outlasted thousands of abler thinkers, and will outlast a thousand more.
>
> —George Bernard Shaw, "Blaming the Bard"
> *Saturday Review*, September 26, 1896

Imminent: likely to occur at any moment.

> Probably the only place where a man can feel really secure is in a maximum security prison, except for the **imminent** threat of release.
>
> —Germaine Greer, "Security"
> *The Female Eunuch* (1970)

120. emulate

verb

To imitate with the intent to equal or surpass.

> Gentlemen, I had hoped you might **emulate** your Saxon forefathers, who thought it not creditable to be unprepared for anything.
>
> —President Woodrow Wilson
> In *Wilson: The Academic Years*
> by Henry W. Bragdon
> President Wilson was speaking to students at Wesleyan University who said they were unprepared for a test.

121. endemic

adjective

Characteristic of or natural to a particular place or people; indigenous; native; belonging exclusively to or confined to a particular place.

> Dr. Hooker has recently shown that in the S.E. corner of Australia, where, apparently, there are many invaders from different quarters of the globe, the **endemic** Australian species have been greatly reduced in number. How much weight to attribute to these several considerations I will not pretend to say; but conjointly they must limit in each country the tendency to an indefinite augmentation of specific forms.
>
> —Charles R. Darwin
> *Origin of Species* (1859)

122. enervate

verb

To render ineffective or inoperative; to deprive of strength or force; to weaken.

Note: Do not confuse ***enervate*** with ***invigorate***. The two words differ significantly, ***enervate*** meaning to deprive of strength, ***invigorate*** to fill with energy and life.

> His musicality is evident in the fresh and lively flow of images, though his tin ear for dialogue and staleness of theme **enervates** the composition.
>
> —Nathan Lee
> Film Review of *The Garden of Earthly Delights* (2003)
> *New York Times*, June 22, 2006

123. enhance

verb

To intensify, to raise to a higher degree, to magnify; to raise the value of.

> Baseball, he determined, would be an excellent hobby. "No sense a man's working his fool head off. I'm going out to the Game three times a week. Besides, fellow ought to support the home team." He did go and support the team, and **enhance** the glory of Zenith, by yelling "Attaboy!" and "Rotten!" He performed the rite scrupulously. He wore a cotton handkerchief about his collar; he became sweaty; he opened his mouth in a wide loose grin; and drank lemon soda out of a bottle. He went to the Game three times a week, for one week.
>
> —Sinclair Lewis
> *Babbitt* (1922)

124. enigma

noun

An inexplicable occurrence or situation, puzzling; a person of puzzling character; a question, saying, or picture with a hidden meaning, a riddle.

> I cannot forecast to you the action of Russia. It is a riddle wrapped in a mystery inside an **enigma**.
>
> —Winston Churchill
> Radio broadcast, October 1, 1939

125. enmity

noun

A feeling or condition of animosity, hatred, ill will.

> Between men and women there is no friendship possible. There is passion, **enmity**, worship, love, but no friendship.
>
> —Oscar Wilde
> *Lady Windermere's Fan* (1892)

126. ennoble

verb

To dignify, to elevate in degree or respect; to exalt; to confer nobility upon.

> [S]uffering does not **ennoble**. It destroys. To resist destruction, self-hatred, or lifelong hopelessness, we have to throw off the conditioning of being despised, the fear of becoming the *they* that is talked about so dismissively, to refuse lying myths and easy moralities, to see ourselves as human, flawed, and extraordinary. All of us—extraordinary.
>
> —Dorothy Allison
> *Skin* (1994)

127. enormity, enormousness

noun

Enormity: outrageous or heinous character; largeness of size, immensity.

Enormousness: largeness of size or scope.

Note: Use *enormousness* when meaning "large" and *enormity* when wishing to emphasize the awfulness of something.

> *Enormity* is frequently used to refer simply to the property of being great in size or extent, but many would prefer that *enormousness* (or a synonym such as *immensity*) be used for this general sense and that *enormity* be limited to situations that demand a negative moral judgment, as in *Not until the war ended and journalists were able to enter Cambodia did the world really become aware of the enormity of Pol Pot's oppression.*
>
> Fifty-nine percent of the Usage Panel rejects the use of *enormity* as a synonym for *immensity* in the sentence *At that point the engineers sat down to design an entirely new viaduct, apparently undaunted by the enormity of their task.* This distinction between *enormity* and *enormousness* has not always existed historically, but nowadays many observe it. Writers who ignore the distinction, as in *the enormity of the President's election victory* or *the enormity of her inheritance*, may find that their words have cast unintended aspersions or evoked unexpected laughter.
>
> —Dictionary.reference.com/browse/enormity

128. epiphany

noun

A sudden appearance or bodily manifestation of a deity; a sudden, intuitive perception of the essential meaning or significance of something, usually initiated by a commonplace occurrence.

Note: The proper noun *Epiphany* names a Christian festival, observed on January 6, to commemorate the manifestation of Christ to the gentiles.

> When we sent our first child off to school I experienced a jarring moment, an **epiphany**. I had been teaching young children for many years, advising parents on a wide range of issues, including the best and most painless ways to separate from their youngsters at school. When my own time came, I found that all my good advice to others was impossible to follow myself.... I felt like a midwife friend of mine who had assisted in the births of hundreds of babies before her own first child was born. In the middle of labor she cried out, "I've told hundreds of women, 'you can do it,' and it can't be done."
>
> —William Ayers
>
> *To Teach: The Journey of a Teacher* (1993)

129. epithet

noun

Any word or phrase applied to a person or thing and used to describe an actual or attributed quality, as in *The Great Communicator* used to describe Ronald Reagan or *man's best friend* used to describe a dog. Also, a term of abuse, as in *racial epithets*, though an epithet need not be derogatory.

> Children, I grant, should be innocent; but when the **epithet** is applied to men, or women, it is but a civil term for weakness.
>
> —Mary Wollstonecraft
> *A Vindication of the Rights of Women* (1792)

130. epitome

noun

A person or thing that is typical of or represents to a high degree the attributes of an entire class; a summary or abstract of a larger literary work.

Note: The word *epitome* does not mean "pinnacle" or "climax" though many people use it this way.

> The three-martini lunch is the **epitome** of American efficiency. Where else can you get an earful, a bellyful and a snootful at the same time?
>
> —Former President Gerald R. Ford
> Speech to the National Restaurant Association
> Chicago, Illinois, May 28, 1978

131. equanimity

noun

Emotional or mental stability or composure, especially when tensed or strained; calm.

> We could not help contrasting the **equanimity** of Nature with the bustle and impatience of man. His words and actions presume always a crisis near at hand, but

> she is forever silent and unpretending.
> —Henry David Thoreau
> "A Walk to Wachusett" (1843)
> *The Writings of Henry David Thoreau* (1906)

132. equity

noun

Characterized by fairness. In law, the term *courts of equity* refers to a parallel system of courts in England and, later, the United States, that could give remedies deemed inadequate in *courts of law*. The term *equitable remedies* refers to forms of relief such as injunctions and orders for specific performance, remedies unavailable under the common law. In finance, *equity* refers to the value of an asset, as in *the equity in your house* (value minus mortgage due).

Note: Below is an English writer commenting on the court of equity. The "Chancellor" is the judge presiding over a court of equity:

> **Equity** is a roguish thing. For Law we have a measure, know what to trust to; **Equity** is according to the conscience of him that is Chancellor, and as that is larger or narrower, so is **Equity**. 'T is all one as if they should make the standard for the measure we call a "foot" a Chancellor's foot; what an uncertain measure would this be! One Chancellor has a long foot, another a short foot, a third an indifferent foot. 'T is the same thing in the Chancellor's conscience.
> —John Selden
> *Table Talk* (1689)

133. equivocate, equivocal

verb

Equivocate: To hedge, to utter ambiguous statements, to use unclear expressions.

adjective

Equivocal: Ambiguous, open to more than one interpretation; often intentionally misleading, as in *an equivocal statement.*

> Elizabeth saw directly that her father had not the smallest intention of yielding; but his answers were at the same time so vague and **equivocal**, that her mother, though often disheartened, had never yet despaired of succeeding at last.
>
> —Jane Austen
> *Pride and Prejudice* (1813)

134. erudition, erudite

noun

Erudition: deep, extensive knowledge and learning.

adjective

Erudite: characterized by great knowledge and learning.

> [Abraham Lincoln] became an **erudite** lawyer, one of the best in Illinois, representing important corporations, presenting cases in the State Supreme Court and appearing before the United States Supreme

> Court. His erudition may have equaled that of many of Ivy League law school graduates.
>
> Lincoln studied English grammar and composition. A copy of a letter he wrote once hung in the Bodleian Library at Oxford, with an inscription below it that read: "The most sublime letter written in the English language." How many courses would Lincoln have needed to write such a letter? Or the Gettysburg address?
>
> —Jules C. Ladenheim
> Letter to the Editor
> *New York Times*, February 13, 1996

135. eschew

verb

To stay away from, to avoid, to abstain from.

> Revelry rules the roost on New Year's Eve, but there are those who value fine dining more than noise-making. Many of Long Island's best restaurants are planning spectacular memory-making feasts for those who want to **eschew** the crowds, drunks, horns and funny hats.
>
> —Joanne Starkey
> "A la Carte: **Eschewing** Foolery"
> *New York Times*, December 18, 1988

136. estimable

adjective

Worthy of respect, deserving esteem and admiration.

> But this is truly a wonderful occasion, the culmination of years of hard work and remarkable generosity, and all of which was due to the good grace of the **estimable** board of trustees of this foundation.
>
> —Former President Ronald Reagan
> Remarks at the ground-breaking
> ceremony for the Reagan Library,
> November 21, 1988

137. euphemism

noun

A figure of speech by which a less offensive phrase is substituted to convey a harsh thought. For example, *pass away* is a euphemism for *die.*

> **Euphemisms** abound for prostitution, but spend a week combing through the phone records of the so-called "D.C. Madam," and it's clear that "call girl" is far and away the most apt. It is all about the calls.
>
> —In "D.C. Madam's" Phone Records,
> "A Slice of Washington"
> CNN.com, July 31, 2007

138. evince

verb

To make manifest or evident; to show clearly, to prove; to reveal the possession of a quality or trait.

> Presidents and prime ministers everywhere, I suspect, sometimes wonder how history will deal with them. Some even **evince** a touch of the insecurity of Thomas Darcy McGee,

an Irish immigrant to Canada who became a father of our confederation.

In one of his poems, McGee, thinking of his birthplace, wrote poignantly, "Am I remembered in Erin? I charge you speak me true. Has my name a sound, a meaning in the scenes my boyhood knew?"

Ronald Reagan will not have to worry about Erin because they remember him well and affectionately there. Indeed they do.

—Former Canadian Prime Minister
Brian Mulroney
Eulogy of Former President
Ronald Reagan, June 11, 2004

139. evoke

verb

To call up or summon forth memories or feelings; to elicit, draw forth; to summon.

Railroad iron is a magician's rod, in its power to **evoke** the sleeping energies of land and water.

—Ralph Waldo Emerson
Speech, Boston, Massachusetts,
February 7, 1844

140. execrable

adjective

Abominable, detestable, abhorrent; very bad.

But is an enemy so **execrable** that though in captivity his wishes and comforts are to

> be disregarded and even crossed? I think not. It is for the benefit of mankind to mitigate the horrors of war as much as possible.
>
> —Thomas Jefferson
> Letter to Patrick Henry, March 27, 1779
> *The Papers of Thomas Jefferson* (1950)

141. expiate

verb

To atone for, to make amends for, as in *to expiate his crimes.*

> "Dolly!" he said, sobbing now; "for mercy's sake, think of the children; they are not to blame! I am to blame, and punish me, make me **expiate** my fault. Anything I can do, I am ready to do anything! I am to blame, no words can express how much I am to blame! But, Dolly, forgive me!"
>
> —Leo Tolstoy
> *Anna Karenin* (1877)

142. explicate

verb

To make clear or plain; to explain, interpret; to develop a theory or principle.

> "This book is about life as it is interpreted by books," Edward Mendelson begins. He takes as his subjects Birth, Childhood, Growth, Marriage, Love, Parenthood and (instead of Death) the Future. The novels he uses to **explicate** his thoughts are . . . novels

> written by women because "the reason that women writers in the nineteenth and twentieth centuries were more likely than men to write about the emotional depths of personal life is that they were more likely to be treated impersonally, to be stereotyped as predictable members of a category, rather than recognized as unique human beings.
>
> —Carolyn See
> Book Review of *The Things That Matter*
> by Edward Mendelson
> *Washington Post*, August 11, 2006

143. extenuate

verb

To diminish the gravity or importance of an offense, fault, or crime; to underestimate, make light of, underrate.

Note: The present participle *extenuating* appears as a verbal adjective to mean to partially excuse, as in *extenuating circumstances*.

> There is a just God who presides over the destinies of nations, and who will raise up friends to fight our battles for us. The battle, sir, is not to the strong alone; it is to the vigilant, the active, the brave.... It is vain, sir, to **extenuate** the matter. Gentlemen may cry, peace, peace—but there is no peace. The war is actually begun! The next gale that sweeps from the north will bring to our ears the clash of resounding arms! Our brethren are already in the field! Why stand we here idle? What is it that gentlemen wish? What

> would they have? Is life so dear, or peace so sweet, as to be purchased at the price of chains and slavery? Forbid it, Almighty God!—I know not what course others may take; but as for me, give me liberty, or give me death!
>
> —Patrick Henry
> Speech to the Virginia Convention,
> Richmond, Virginia,
> March 23, 1775

144. extricate

verb

To release or free from entanglement, to disengage, usually from a situation.

> Tell a man whose house is on fire to give a moderate alarm; tell him to moderately rescue his wife from the hands of the ravisher; tell the mother to gradually **extricate** her babe from the fire into which it has fallen; but urge me not to use moderation in a case like the present.
>
> —William Lloyd Garrison
> *The Liberator*, January 1, 1831

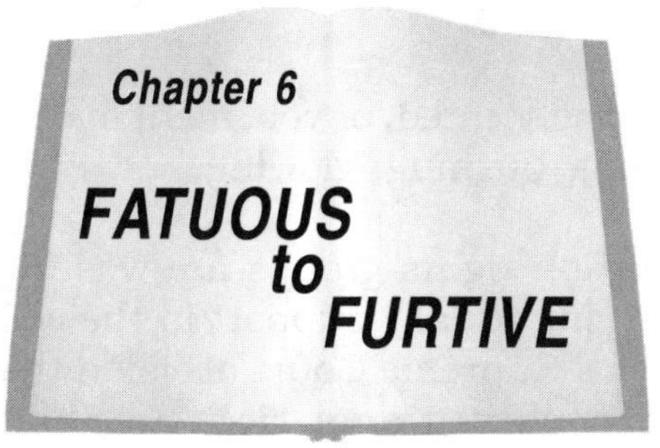

145. fatuous

adjective

Foolish, inane, silly, especially in a self-satisfied way.

> I'm sick of the Powder Room. I'm sick of pretending that some **fatuous** male's self-important pronouncements are the objects of my undivided attention, I'm sick of going to films and plays when someone else wants to, and sick of having no opinions of my own about either. I'm sick of being a transvestite. I refuse to be a female impersonator. I am a woman, not a castrate.
>
> —Germaine Greer
> "Soul: The Stereotype"
> *The Female Eunuch* (1970)

146. fervor, fervid

noun

Fervor: great warmth or earnestness of feeling; intense heat.

adjective

Fervid: intense, heated, or vehement in enthusiasm; intensely hot, burning, glowing.

> Abortion rights groups are wasting no time in trying to rally support in the wake of last week's Supreme Court decision that upheld the constitutional right to abortion but permitted states to enact restrictions.
>
> **Fervid** television commercials and newspaper advertisements, as well as strongly worded direct-mail appeals, are appearing that interpret the Court's narrowly decided verdict in the most apocalyptic terms.
>
> —Stuart Elliott
> "Fervid Appeals on Abortion
> Follow High Court Decision"
> *New York Times*, July 7, 1992

147. foible

noun

A minor failing or weakness of character; slight defect or flaw.

> It is the **foible** especially of American youth—pretension. The mark of the man of the world is absence of pretension. He does not make a speech, he takes a low business-tone, avoids all brag, is nobody, dresses plainly, promises not at all, performs much, speaks in monosyllables, hugs his fact. He calls his employment by its lowest name, and so takes

> from evil tongues their sharpest weapon. His conversation clings to the weather and the news, yet he allows himself to be surprised into thought, and the unlocking of his learning and philosophy.
>
> —Ralph Waldo Emerson "Culture"
> *The Conduct of Life* (1860)

148. forego, forgo

verb

Forego: to go before, precede. The past tense is *forewent*, the past participle *foregone.*

Forgo: to refrain from, to do without; to give up, renounce. The past tense is *forwent*, the past participle *forgone.*

Note: Consider the following discussion from Bryan Garner's *The Oxford Dictionary of American Usage and Style* (2000):

> Although a few apologists argue that these words are interchangeable, they have separate histories. And their meanings are so different that it's worth preserving the distinction. *Forego*, as suggested by the prefix, means "to go before." *Forgo* means "to do without; pass up voluntarily; waive; renounce."

Mr. Garner then shows how leading newspapers use incorrect spellings, quoting passages from the *Los Angeles Times* and the *Boston Herald.* Below is an example of the *New York Times* using *forewent* when it meant *forwent*:

> [Don Ameche] had a natural gift for acting and got his first professional opportunity when he filled in for a missing lead in the stock theater production of *Excess Baggage*. After that, he **forewent** [sic] his law career and became a full-time theatrical actor.
>
> —Sandra Brennan, Biography of Don Ameche in "All Movie Guide" *New York Times*, movies.nytimes.com/ person/1323/Don-Ameche/biography

149. fungible

adjective

Usually used to describe goods of a nature or kind that may be freely exchangeable or replaceable for others of like kind or nature. In finance, *fungible assets* refers to securities or commodities that are freely mixed and whose ownership is not specifically assigned to particular entities.

> I am a retired certified public accountant who audited a New York State school district the first year in which money collected from the sale of lottery tickets went to education.
>
> My audit showed that in fact the money from the lottery was **fungible**: the money the school gained from the lottery was canceled out by other cutbacks in state aid.
>
> —Myron Heckler
> Letter to the Editor
> *New York Times*, April 2, 1999

150. farther, further

adjective, adverb
Farther: the comparative form of the adjective and adverb *far*; often followed by *than.*

Further: may be used in the adverbial sense of "moreover," as in *Further, you hurt my feelings*; in the adjectival sense of "more extended," as in *no further comment*, and of "additional," *Further bulletins came in.* Also, only *further* can act as a verb, as in *He wants to further his career.*

Note: Although some usage guides insist that only *farther* should be used for physical distance (We walked *farther* than we planned), *farther* and *further* have been used interchangeably throughout much of their histories.

—http://dictionary.reference.com/search?q=farther

"Parcells Decides to Return, but Heads **Farther** South"
—*New York Times* Headline
December 20, 2007

"The Primary, Upon **Further** Dissection"
—*New York Times* Headline
January 11, 2008

151. furtive

adjective

Done or taken or used surreptitiously, on the sly; shifty.

We are a sad lot, the cell biologists. Like the **furtive** collectors of stolen art, we are forced to be lonely admirers of spectacular architecture, exquisite symmetry, dramas of violence and death, mobility, self-sacrifice and, yes, rococo sex.

—Lorraine Lee Cudmore
The Center of Life, Quadrangle 77
Science Digest, November 1977

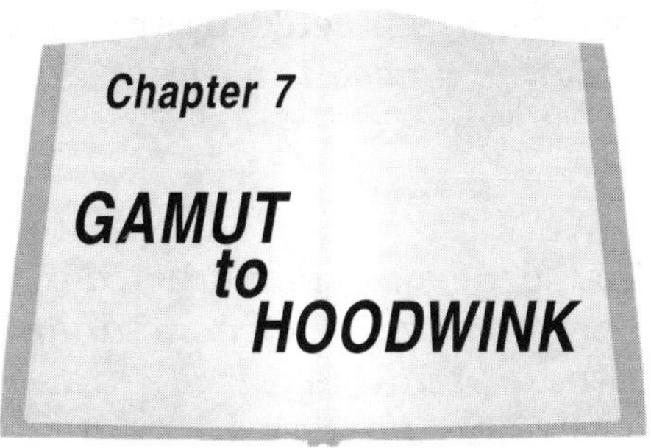

152. gamut

noun

The whole range, sequence, or scale, as in *the gamut of emotion from joy to grief.*

Note: Way too often you will hear people say *runs the gambit.* Careful. It's *run the gamut.*

> Photography records the **gamut** of feelings written on the human face, the beauty of the earth and skies that man has inherited and the wealth and confusion man has created.
>
> —Edward Steichen
> *Time*, April 7, 1961

153. generic

adjective

Referring to or applicable to all members of a group, kind, or class. In biology, of or referring to a genus.

In law, a word not protected by trademark, as in *The word "cola" is a generic term.*

noun

A type of food, drug, or item marketed in a package without a brand name. A *generic drug* is one on which the patent has expired, manufactured according to the patent by a *generic drug manufacturer.*

> "Mother" has always been a **generic** term synonymous with love, devotion, and sacrifice. There's always been something mystical and reverent about them. They're the Walter Cronkites of the human race . . . infallible, virtuous, without flaws and conceived without original sin, with no room for ambivalence.
>
> —Erma Bombeck
> *Motherhood, The Second Oldest Profession* (1983)

154. germane

adjective

Significantly or closely related, relevant, pertinent.

> Quotes from Mao, Castro, and Che Guevara . . . are as **germane** to our highly technological, computerized society as a stagecoach on a jet runway at Kennedy airport.
>
> —Saul Alinsky
> *Rules for Radicals* (1971)

155. gregarious

adjective
Fond of the company of others, sociable; pertaining to animals, living in herds or flocks.

> New York is the greatest city in the world for lunch . . . That's the **gregarious** time. And when that first martini hits the liver like a silver bullet, there is a sigh of contentment that can be heard in Dubuque.
>
> —William Emerson, Jr.
> *Newsweek*, December 29, 1975

156. grizzly, grisly

adjective

Grizzly: grayish; also, as a noun, a large bear.

Grisly: causing a feeling of horror; gruesome; horrible, as in *a grisly murder.*

> I often look upon a face
> Most ugly, **grisly**, bare and thin;
> I often view the hollow place,
> Where eyes and nose had sometimes been.
>
> —Robert Southwell (1561–1595)
> "Upon the Image of Death"

157. hackney

verb

To make stale or trite by frequent use or repetition.

Note: As a noun, *hackney* means a carriage or coach for hire. As a proper noun, *Hackney* is an English breed of horses with high-stepping gaits. As a verbal adjective, *hackneyed* means banal or trite because of frequent use or repetition.

> The Americans . . . have invented so wide a range of pithy and **hackneyed** phrases that they can carry on an amusing and animated conversation without giving a moment's reflection to what they are saying and so leave their minds free to consider the more important matters of big business and fornication.
>
> —W. Somerset Maugham
> *Cakes and Ale* (1930)

158. halcyon

adjective

Calm, peaceful, as in *halcyon weather*; rich, wealthy, as in *halcyon days of peace*; happy, carefree, as in *the halcyon days of our youth.*

> It was a **halcyon** day, and as they neared the shore and the salt breezes scurried by, he began to picture the ocean and long, level stretches of sand and red roofs over blue sea. Then they hurried through the little town and it all flashed upon his consciousness to a mighty pæan of emotion.
>
> —F. Scott Fitzgerald
> *This Side of Paradise* (1920)

159. harass

verb

To bother continually; to torment, usually with troubles or cares; to pester.

Note: You may pronounce it either way, with an accent on the first syllable or the last. In American English, the better pronunciation accents the second syllable.

> Here is a fairly simple proposition: Women should never be subjected to sexual harassment anywhere. That includes state property. Yet crowds of men continue to **harass** women at Jets' games in the Meadowlands sports complex.
>
> —"Zero Tolerance on Harassment"
> Editorial in *New York Times*,
> December 16, 2007

160. harbinger

noun

One who or that which foreruns and announces the coming of any person or thing; anything that foreshadows a coming thing or event.

> Now the bright morning star, day's **harbinger**,
> Comes dancing from the east, and leads with her
> The flow'ry May, who from her green lap throws

> The yellow cowslip and the pale primrose.
> Hail, bounteous May, that dost inspire
> Mirth and youth and warm desire!
>
> —John Milton
> "On May Morning"
> *Milton's Poetical Works* (1966)

161. heinous

adjective

Odious, hateful, totally reprehensible.

> If you commit a big crime then you are crazy, and the more **heinous** the crime the crazier you must be. Therefore you are not responsible, and nothing is your fault.
>
> —Peggy Noonan
> Commenting on the insanity verdict handed down to John Hinckley, would-be assassin of President Reagan in 1981, as reported by Ms. Noonan and Dan Rather.
> *What I Saw at the Revolution* (1990)

162. homogeneous

adjective

Composed of elements or parts of the same kind; essentially alike.

> Israel's new deputy prime minister on Sunday called for a near-total separation between Arabs and Jews in the Holy Land, sparking a wave of condemnation less than

> a week after the far-right politician joined the Cabinet.
>
> —Ravi Nessman
> "Israeli Official Wants **Homogenous** Nation"
> *Washington Post*, November 5, 2006

163. hoodwink

verb

To deceive, trick, cheat, swindle.

> British spy chiefs have grave doubts that Iran has mothballed its nuclear weapons programme, as a US intelligence report claimed last week, and believe the CIA has been **hoodwinked** by Teheran.
>
> —Tim Shipman, Philip Sherwell, and Carolynne Wheeler
> "Iran **'hoodwinked'** CIA over Nuclear Plans"
> *The Telegraph*, December 12, 2007

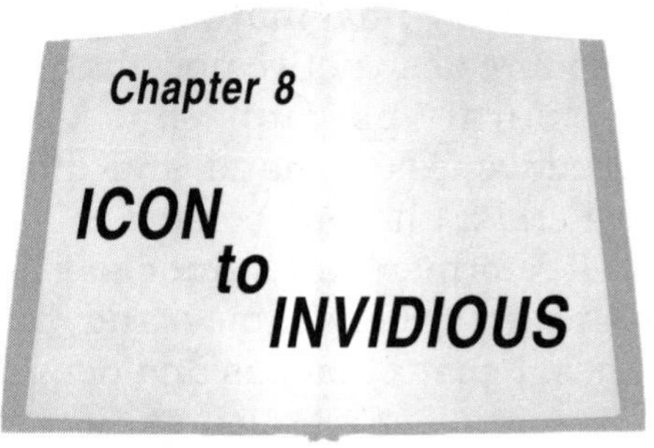

164. icon, iconoclast

noun

Icon: An image, picture, likeness, or representation; an enduring symbol; a person who is the object of devotion or attention. In the computer world, a graphical image or symbol on a screen that represents an underlying file or program.

> "Grilled cheese sandwich: Updating an American **Icon**"
>
> A grilled cheese sandwich is an ode to childhood, a purist's dream and an archetypal comfort food all at once. Just three mundane ingredients and a few minutes should be all it takes to create something downright sublime, right? So why do so few sublime ones come our way?
>
> —Amy Scattergood
> *Los Angeles Times*, August 8, 2007

Iconoclast: One who attacks or destroys cherished beliefs or symbols. Originally, in the eighth and ninth centuries, the *iconoclasts* were those who literally destroyed paintings and sculptures.

> You have no imagination, Ann. I am ten times more destructive now than I was then. The moral passion has taken my destructiveness in hand and directed it to moral ends. I have become a reformer, and, like all reformers, an **iconoclast**. I no longer break cucumber frames and burn gorse bushes: I shatter creeds and demolish idols.
>
> —George Bernard Shaw
> *Man and Superman* (1903)

165. idiosyncrasy

noun

A characteristic, mental quality, or habit peculiar to an individual or group.

> "What's to be done? Here's the cottage, taking one time with another, will produce, say seventy pounds a year. I think we may safely put it down at that. Well!—That's all we've got," said my aunt; with whom it was an **idiosyncrasy**, as it is with some horses, to stop very short when she appeared to be in a fair way of going on for a long while.
>
> —Charles Dickens
> *David Copperfield* (1850)

166. imbroglio

noun

A misunderstanding or disagreement attended by ill feeling, perplexity, or strife.

> In 1807, the US government implemented the Embargo Act. This decree, which closed

American ports to foreign trade and prevented US ships from leaving those ports, was extremely unpopular because it hurt America more than it did Britain or France. Two years later, Jefferson retired and left the foreign policy **imbroglio** to the new president, James Madison.

—galafilm.com/1812/e/people/jefferson.html

167. immutable

adjective

Unchangeable; not subject or susceptible to change.

> Despite the promised "new direction for America," getting the money out of politics and all of that, some facts of Washington life appear **immutable** and eternal.
>
> "One hundred hours to make this the most honest and open Congress in history," House Speaker Nancy Pelosi declared at the beginning of a history-making day—which ended last night with the Democrat from California presiding over a glitzy fundraiser open to anyone with $1,000 for a ticket.
>
> —David Montgomery and J. Freedom du Lac, "House Warming" *Washington Post*, January 5, 2007

168. impalpable

adjective

Incapable of being perceived by the sense of touch;

intangible; difficult for the mind to grasp easily or readily, as in *impalpable distinctions*.

> This name [Virginia Woolf] springs to one's mind because Miss [Nadine] Gordimer is a writer who can not only capture but express in the lives of human beings those moments which are so fleeting, so **impalpable**, as well as so common that they are overlooked by all but a very rare artist. I can think of no modern first "novel" superior to Miss Gordimer's.
>
> —James Stern
> "Out of Rags and Hovels"
> Book review of *The Lying Days*
> by Nadine Gordimer
> *New York Times*, October 4, 1953

169. impecunious

adjective

Having little or no money; penniless; poor.

> He was an eccentric, disheveled, toothless and **impecunious** lifelong bachelor, an amateur poet and musician and an autodidact able to converse knowledgeably with experts in many different fields. And he was a genius draftsman, one of 18th-century France's greatest. That's Gabriel de Saint-Aubin (1724-80), the subject of a gripping exhibition at the Frick Collection.
>
> —Ken Johnson
> "Forever Drawing the World in All Its Minuscule Detail"
> *New York Times*, November 2, 2007

170. impervious

adjective

Impenetrable, as in *impervious to rain*; incapable of being injured or impaired, as in *impervious to wear and tear*; incapable of being persuaded, influenced, or affected, as in *impervious to another person's suffering.*

> Over the past several years, car buyers have been spoiled by the generous cash-back and low-interest offers that dealers were slapping on pretty much any car in the lot.
>
> "People became addicted, but also **impervious** to those incentives," says Robert Gentile, director of car information products at *Consumer Reports*. As incentives became a less-effective marketing tool to drive buyers to the dealerships, the manufacturers naturally tried to trim wide-scale promotions. This was yet another reason for the sales slump this summer.
>
> —Aleksandra Todorova
> "Timing a Car Purchase"
> *Wall Street Journal*, August 26, 2007

171. implicate, implicit

verb

Implicate: to show to be also involved, usually in an incriminating manner, as in *He was implicated in the crime*; to imply as a necessary circumstance, or as something to be inferred or understood; to connect or relate to intimately; affect as a consequence, as in *The malfunctioning of one part of the system implicates another part.*

> Federal prosecutors are investigating whether two contractors **implicated** in the bribery of former Rep. Randall "Duke" Cunningham supplied him with prostitutes and free use of a limousine and hotel suites, pursuing evidence that could broaden their long-running inquiry.
>
> —Scot J. Paltrow
> "Prosecutors May Widen Congressional-Bribe Case"
> *Wall Street Journal*, April 27, 2006

adjective

Implicit: implied rather than expressed, as in *an implicit understanding*; unreserved and unquestioning, absolute, as in *his implicit trust in his boss*; potentially contained in, as in *the danger implicit in the new venture.*

> Even more striking, Justice O'Connor all but invited the Administration to set up a military court to hear Hamdi's plea. That suggestion goes a bridge farther than even President Bush has dared. His controversial 2001 order establishing military tribunals to try enemy combatants specifically excluded U.S. citizens even though there is ample legal precedent for their use. The Court's ruling is also an **implicit** suggestion that the military is capable of adequately reviewing challenges brought by the Gitmo prisoners.
>
> —"Terror and the Court"
> Editorial in *Wall Street Journal*,
> June 29, 2004

172. importune

verb

To beset with solicitations, to demand with urgency; to beg for something urgently.

> When Benedict comes to the United States, he is likely to be **importuned** by conservative Catholics to side with the hard-liners. He would be wiser to listen to other Catholics, laypeople as well as clergy, who know what mischief would be caused by a decree that would seem to force some Catholic officials to choose between their responsibility to their constituents or the Constitution and their standing in the church.
>
> — "Teaching the Pope"
> Editorial in *Los Angeles Times*,
> November 14, 2007

173. improvident

adjective

Lacking foresight; incautious; neglecting to provide for future needs.

> In the House of Representatives late this afternoon a sensational appeal was made by Representative John J. Fitzgerald of New York to vote against **improvident** and improper appropriations before it was too late for them to stop the conduct of which the Democratic members "have been guilty."
>
> —"Warns Democrats to Stop Waste;
> Becoming the Laughing Stock of the Country

Through Improvidence, Says Fitzgerald"
New York Times, April 11, 1914

174. impugn

verb

To challenge as false, cast doubt upon.

> "This was a great N.Y.P.D. officer who dedicated himself—put his life in harm's way hundreds of times during his career—and you can use your own definition," Mr. [Michael R.] Bloomberg said at a news conference in Brooklyn when asked if he regretted his earlier comments. "It's a question of how you want to define what a hero is, and certainly I did not mean to hurt the family or **impugn** his reputation."
>
> —Diane Cardwell
> "Mayor Backs Away From Questioning Dead Officer's Heroism"
> *New York Times*, October 31, 2007

175. impute

verb

To ascribe or attribute, as in *She imputed special powers to the new software program.*

> Kings are much to be pitied, who, misled by weak ministers, and deceived by wicked favourites, run into political errors, which involve their families in ruin: and it might prove some solace to his present majesty, when, fallen from the head of the greatest

empire the world has seen, he shall again exhibit in the political system of Europe the original character of a petty king of Britain, could he **impute** his fall to error alone. Error is to be pitied and pardoned: it is the weakness of human nature. But vice is a foul blemish, not pardonable in any character.

—Thomas Jefferson
"Refutation of the Argument that the Colonies Were Established at the Expense of the British Nation" (1775)
The Papers of Thomas Jefferson (1950)

176. inane

adjective

Lacking sense, ideas, or significance; silly; empty or void.

Anna made no answer. The conductor and her two fellow-passengers did not notice under her veil her panic-stricken face. She went back to her corner and sat down. The couple seated themselves on the opposite side, and intently but surreptitiously scrutinised her clothes. Both husband and wife seemed repulsive to Anna. The husband asked, would she allow him to smoke, obviously not with a view to smoking but to getting into conversation with her. Receiving her assent, he said to his wife in French something about caring less to smoke than to talk. They made **inane** and affected remarks to one another, entirely for her

> benefit. Anna saw clearly that they were sick of each other, and hated each other. And no one could have helped hating such miserable monstrosities.
>
> —Leo Tolstoy
> *Anna Karenin* (1877)

177. inanimate

adjective

Lacking the qualities associated with living organisms; sluggish, dull.

> "Do you call that happiness—the ownership of human beings?" cried Miss Stackpole. "He owns his tenants, and he has thousands of them. It is pleasant to own something, but **inanimate** objects are enough for me. I don't insist on flesh and blood, and minds and consciences."
>
> —Henry James
> *The Portrait of a Lady* (1908)

178. inchoate

adjective

Not yet completed or fully developed; just begun, incipient; not organized, lacking order.

> Until an employee has earned his retirement pay...[it] is but an **inchoate** right.
>
> —*Peterson v. Fire & Police Pension Association* (1988)

179. incipient

adjective

Beginning to appear or exist, in an initial stage, as in *an incipient disease.*

> [Brent] Scowcroft predicted "an **incipient** civil war" would grip Iraq and said the best hope for pulling the country from chaos would be to turn the U.S. operation over to NATO or the United Nations—which, he said, would not be so hostilely viewed by Iraqis.
>
> —Dana Priest and Robin Wright
> "Scowcroft Skeptical Vote Will Stabilize Iraq"
> *Washington Post,* January 7, 2005

180. indolent

adjective

Laziness; having or showing a disposition to avoid exertion or work. In pathology, causing little or no pain, as in *an indolent sore slow to heal.*

> Miss Bingley was engrossed by Mr. Darcy, her sister scarcely less so; and as for Mr. Hurst, by whom Elizabeth sat, he was an **indolent** man, who lived only to eat, drink, and play at cards, who, when he found her prefer a plain dish to a ragout, had nothing to say to her.
>
> —Jane Austen
> *Pride and Prejudice* (1813)

181. ineffable

adjective

Incapable of being expressed or described in words, as in *ineffable joy;* not to be spoken because of its sacredness, unutterable, as in *the ineffable name of the deity.*

> He began with being a young man of promise; at Oxford he distinguished himself, to his father's **ineffable** satisfaction, and the people about him said it was a thousand pities so clever a fellow should be shut out from a career.
>
> —Henry James
> *The Portrait of a Lady* (1908)

182. inexorable

adjective

Unalterable, unyielding, as in *an inexorable truth*; unrelenting, not to be moved, persuaded, affected by entreaties or prayers, as in *an inexorable bill collector.*

> And never has this lesson been taught with sterner and more unpitying force than by the author of "Anna Karenin." "Vengeance is mine, and I will repay," is the motto prefixed to the novel. And as we read the story, we feel throughout the overhanging presence of an **inexorable** power that shapes out the lives of men, allotting to them peace or discord, according as they submit to or rebel against their fate.
>
> —Charles E. Turner

Review of *Anna Karenin* by Leo Tolstoy
Criticisms and Interpretations (1917)

183. infer, imply

verb

Infer: to derive by reasoning, to conclude or judge from evidence or premises.
Imply: to suggest or indicate a conclusion without its being explicitly stated; to involve as a necessary circumstance, as in *speech implies a speaker.*

Note: *Infer* is sometimes confused with *imply*, but the distinction is a useful one. When we say that a speaker or sentence *implies* something, we mean that it is conveyed or suggested without being stated outright: *When the mayor said that she would not rule out a business tax increase, she implied* (not *inferred*) *that some taxes might be raised.* Inference, on the other hand, is the activity performed by a reader or interpreter in drawing conclusions that are not explicit in what is said: *When the mayor said that she would not rule out a tax increase, we inferred that she had been consulting with some new financial advisers, since her old advisers were in favor of tax reductions.*

—Dictionary.reference.com/
browse/infer

184. infuse

verb

To instill, introduce, or inculcate principles or qualities, as if by pouring, as in *The teacher infused new life into the classroom*; to inspire or imbue (usually followed by *with*), as in *The new coach infused the team with enthusiasm.*

> "Oh yes, that is what prevented me from feeling sleepy. I think I should have no other mortal wants, if I could always have plenty of music. It seems to **infuse** strength into my limbs, and ideas into my brain. Life seems to go on without effort, when I am filled with music. At other times one is conscious of carrying a weight."
>
> —George Eliot
> *The Mill on the Floss* (1860)

185. ingenuous, disingenuous

adjective

Ingenuous: candid, frank, or open in character or quality; characterized by an inability to mask feelings, not devious.

Disingenuous: the *dis-* prefix establishes the negative; thus, not candid, not frank, not open in character or quality; insincere.

Note: The meaning of *disingenuous* has been shifting about lately, as if people were unsure of its proper meaning. Generally, it means "insincere" and often seems to be a synonym of *cynical* or *calculating.* Not surprisingly, the word is used often in political contexts, as in *It is both insensitive and disingenuous for the White House to describe its aid package and the proposal to eliminate the federal payment as "tough love."* This use of the word is accepted by 94 percent of the Usage Panel. Most

Panelists also accept the extended meaning relating to less reproachable behavior. Fully 88 percent accept *disingenuous* with the meaning "playfully insincere, faux-naïf," as in the example *"I don't have a clue about late Beethoven!" he said. The remark seemed disingenuous, coming from one of the world's foremost concert pianists.* Sometimes *disingenuous* is used as a synonym for *naive,* as if the *dis-* prefix functioned as an intensive (as it does in certain words like *disannul*) rather than as a negative element. This usage does not find much admiration among Panelists, however. Seventy-five percent do not accept it in the phrase *a disingenuous tourist who falls prey to stereotypical con artists.*

—Dictionary.reference.com/browse/disingenuous

186. ingratiate

verb

To win confidence or good graces for oneself, especially through deliberate effort.

> "Yes, this is a monument he is setting up here," said Anna, turning to Dolly with that sly smile of comprehension with which she had previously talked about the hospital.
>
> "Oh, it's a work of real importance!" said Sviazhsky. But to show he was not trying to **ingratiate** himself with Vronsky, he promptly added some slightly critical remarks.
>
> —Leo Tolstoy
> *Anna Karenin* (1877)

187. inimical

adjective

Adverse in effect or tendency, harmful, unfavorable; unfriendly, hostile.

> In other words, Mr. Dimmesdale, whose sensibility of nerve often produced the effect of spiritual intuition, would become vaguely aware that something **inimical** to his peace had thrust itself into relation with him. But Old Roger Chillingworth, too, had perceptions that were almost intuitive; and when the minister threw his startled eyes towards him, there the physician sat, his kind, watchful, sympathising, but never intrusive friend.
>
> —Nathaniel Hawthorne
> *The Scarlet Letter* (1850)

188. insatiable

adjective

Incapable of being satisfied or appeased, as in *an insatiable thirst for fine wine.*

> Sonia said this as though in despair, wringing her hands in excitement and distress. Her pale cheeks flushed, there was a look of anguish in her eyes. It was clear that she was stirred to the very depths, that she was longing to speak, to champion, to express something. A sort of **insatiable** compassion, if one may so express it, was

> reflected in every feature of her face.
>
> —Fyodor Dostoevsky
> *Crime and Punishment* (1917)

189. inscrutable

adjective

Incapable of being analyzed, investigated, or scrutinized; impenetrable, not easily understood; unfathomable; mysterious, as in *an inscrutable smile*; incapable of being seen through, as in *the inscrutable depths of the ocean.*

> We have as yet hardly spoken of the infant: that little creature, whose innocent life had sprung, by **inscrutable** decree of Providence, a lovely and immortal flower, out of the rank luxuriance of a guilty passion. How strange it seemed to the sad woman, as she watched the growth, and the beauty that became every day more brilliant, and the intelligence that threw its quivering sunshine over the tiny features of this child! Her Pearl!—for so had Hester called her; not as a name expressive of her aspect, which had nothing of the calm, white, unimpassioned lustre that would be indicated by the comparison. But she named the infant "Pearl," as being of great price—purchased with all she had—her mother's only treasure!
>
> —Nathaniel Hawthorne
> *The Scarlet Letter* (1850)

190. insidious

adjective

Intended to beguile or entrap, as in *an insidious plot*; stealthily deceitful or treacherous, as in *an insidious foe*; proceeding in a seemingly harmless way but actually with dangerous effect, as in *an insidious disease.*

> She was terror-stricken by the revelations that were thus made. What were they? Could they be other than the **insidious** whispers of the bad angel, who would fain have persuaded the struggling woman, as yet only half his victim, that the outward guise of purity was but a lie, and that, if truth were everywhere to be shown, a scarlet letter would blaze forth on many a bosom besides Hester Prynne's?
>
> —Nathaniel Hawthorne
> *The Scarlet Letter* (1850)

191. insipid

adjective

Lacking interesting, stimulating, or distinctive qualities, as in *an insipid, boring speaker*; without a sufficient taste to be pleasing, as in *an insipid meal.*

> Kitty, to her very material advantage, spent the chief of her time with her two elder sisters. In society so superior to what she had generally known, her improvement was great. She was not of so ungovernable a temper as Lydia; and, removed from the influence of Lydia's example, she became, by proper attention and management, less irritable, less ignorant, and less **insipid**.

From the further disadvantage of Lydia's society she was of course carefully kept; and though Mrs. Wickham frequently invited her to come and stay with her, with the promise of balls and young men, her father would never consent to her going.

—Jane Austen
Pride and Prejudice (1813)

192. intrepid

adjective

Fearless, courageous, and bold.

Unchecked, the tourist will climb over the fence and come right into your house to take pictures of you in your habitat. Cities mindful of tourists have built elaborate "tourist traps" which, luckily, work. Tourists are kept confined to these, and few escape. There is, of course, the type known as the "**intrepid** tourist." This one has to be watched carefully or he can become most annoying. Little wonder these are so often the target of terrorists. If there is an aspect of benign terror about the tourist, there is also a great deal of tourist in the terrorist. Terrorists travel with only one thing in mind, just like the tourist, and the specifics of places escape them both. Terrorists travel for the purpose of shooting unsuspecting foreigners, just as tourists travel for the purpose of shooting them with a camera.

—Andrei Codrescu
"The Tourist"
Raised by Puppets (1990)

193. intrinsic

adjective

Belonging to a thing by its nature, inherent, as in *the intrinsic value of gold.*

> And yet, beyond that, she hardly knew what he had—save of course his **intrinsic** qualities. Oh, he was **intrinsic** enough; she never thought of his even looking for artificial aids.
>
> —Henry James
> *The Portrait of a Lady* (1908)

194. invective

noun

An utterance intended to cast censure or reproach; vehement denunciation; an insulting word or utterance.

> The art of **invective** resembles the art of boxing. Very few fights are won with the straight left. It is too obvious, and it can be too easily countered. The best punches, like the best pieces of **invective** in this style, are either short-arm jabs, unexpectedly rapid and deadly; or else one-two blows, where you prepare your opponent with the first hit, and then, as his face comes forward, connect with your other fist: one, two. Both are effective; but they can be administered only by a real artist, with a real wish to knock his enemy out.

—Gilbert Highet
"The Art of Invective"
A Clerk of Oxenford: Essays on Literature and Life (1954)

195. inveigh

verb

To utter vehement censure or invective, to protest strongly (often followed by *against*).

> Senate Democrats who oppose President Bush's Iraq policy spoke today against Condoleezza Rice's nomination to be secretary of state, signaling that they intended to vigorously oppose the administration's foreign policy despite their minority status.
>
> —David Stout
> "Democrats Use Rice Debate to **Inveigh** Against War in Iraq"
> *New York Times*, January 25, 2005

196. invidious

adjective

Calculated to cause ill will or resentment; hateful, as in *invidious remarks*; offensively or unfairly injurious, as in *invidious discrimination*; tending to cause animosity.

> The **invidious** effects of such mass, roundup urinalysis is that it casually sweeps up the innocent with the guilty.
>
> —Judge H. Lee Sarokin,

U.S. District Court, New Jersey
Ruling that mandatory testing of
government employees to determine
presence of illegal drugs is
unconstitutional, September 18, 1986

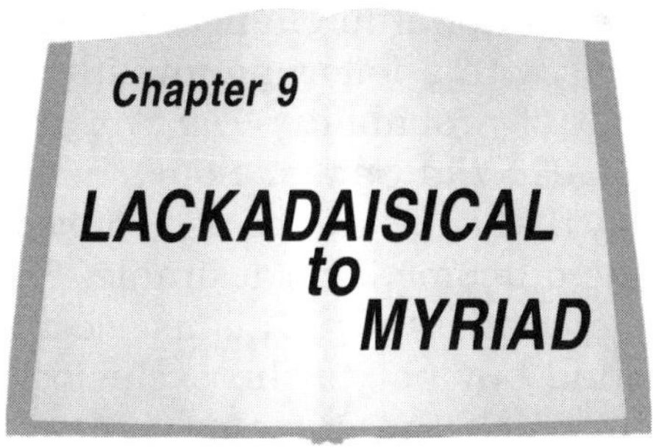

197. lackadaisical

adjective

Without vigor, determination, or interest; lethargic; listless; indolent.

Note: This word is not pronounced with an *x*, as in *laxadaisical.* Start the word with *lack.*

> Those who stop obey orders. Able-bodied, clean-minded women we want also—mothers and teachers. No **lackadaisical** ladies—no blasted rolling eyes. We can't have any weak or silly. Life is real again, and the useless and cumbersome and mischievous have to die. They ought to die. They ought to be willing to die.
>
> —H. G. Wells
> *The War of the Worlds* (1898)

198. liable, libel

adjective

Liable: legally responsible; subject or susceptible to; likely or apt.

Note: *Liable* is often interchangeable with *likely* in constructions with a following infinitive where the sense is that of probability: *The Sox are liable* (or *likely*) *to sweep the Series.* Some usage guides, however, say that *liable* can be used only in contexts in which the outcome is undesirable: *The picnic is liable to be spoiled by rain.* This use occurs often in formal writing but not to the exclusion of use in contexts in which the outcome is desirable: *The drop in unemployment is liable to stimulate the economy. Apt* may also be used in place of *liable* or *likely* in all the foregoing examples.

—dictionary.reference.com/
browse/liable

noun

Libel: the legal tort of defamation, which occurs in the written word; efamation in the oral word is *slander.* Thus, one can be *liable* for *libel.*

199. literal

adjective

Involving or being the strict or primary meaning of the word or words; not figurative; not metaphorical; actual or factual, not exaggerated.

Note: Many people use *literal* when they don't mean it, as in *We were literally dead from exhaustion.*

> *Anna Karenin* is the most widely known of Tolstoy's works and is generally regarded as his artistic masterpiece. It exhibits favorably his peculiar realism—a realism which consists not merely in the accuracy of **literal** description of actual types and conditions,

but in an essential truthfulness which refuses to yield to the pressure of doctrine or the enticements of sentiment.

—Biographical Note by William Allan Neilson in *Anna Karenin* by Leo Tolstoy P.F. Collier & Son, 1917 edition

200. loquacious

adjective

Talkative, tending to talk too much, chattering, babbling, garrulous.

I found it not difficult, in the excitement of Mr. Chillip's own brain, under his potations of negus, to divert his attention from this topic to his own affairs, on which, for the next half-hour, he was quite **loquacious**; giving me to understand, among other pieces of information, that he was then at the Gray's Inn Coffee-house to lay his professional evidence before a Commission of Lunacy, touching the state of mind of a patient who had become deranged from excessive drinking.

—Charles Dickens
David Copperfield (1850)

201. macrocosm

noun

The great universe or world, the universe considered as a whole; the total complex structure of something.

This monster of a land, this mightiest of

> nations, this spawn of the future, turns out to be the **macrocosm** of microcosm me.
>
> —John Steinbeck
> *Travels With Charley: In Search of America* (1962)

202. magnanimous

adjective

Generous in treating or judging others, generous in forgiving an insult; free from petty vindictiveness; noble, high-minded.

> Vronsky felt his elevation and his own abasement, his truth and his own falsehood. He felt that the husband was **magnanimous** even in his sorrow, while he had been base and petty in his deceit. But this sense of his own humiliation before the man he had unjustly despised made up only a small part of his misery.
>
> —Leo Tolstoy
> *Anna Karenin* (1877)

203. maudlin

adjective

Foolishly sentimental; tearfully and weakly emotional.

> The young ladies did not drink it; Osborne did not like it; and the consequence was that Jos, that fat *gourmand,* drank up the whole contents of the bowl; and the consequence

> of his drinking up the whole contents of the bowl was a liveliness which at first was astonishing, and then became almost painful; for he talked and laughed so loud as to bring scores of listeners round the box, much to the confusion of the innocent party within it; and, volunteering to sing a song (which he did in that **maudlin** high key peculiar to gentlemen in an inebriated state), he almost drew away the audience who were gathered round the musicians in the gilt scollop-shell, and received from his hearers a great deal of applause.
>
> —William M. Thackeray
> *Vanity Fair* (1847–48)

204. mendacious

adjective

Untrue, false; habitually telling lies, dishonest.

> For the last week, I've been intimately involved with Jack Nicholson. He's both a charmer and a cliché. Passionate about truth in his art and a **mendacious** hypocrite in real life. Wildly generous, yet appallingly parsimonious. A pothead and a fine art collector. A priapic satyr and a romantic fool. I now have a singular insight into Nicholson. But I haven't a clue about the real man behind the joker's mask.
>
> —Tara Ison
> Book Review of *Five Easy Decades* by Dennis McDougal
> *Los Angeles Times*, November 22, 2007

205. meretricious

adjective
Showy, gaudy, tawdry; deceptively pleasing, based on pretense; also relating to a prostitute, as in *a meretricious relationship.*

> "She is charming," thought Eugène, more and more in love. He looked round him at the room; there was an ostentatious character about the luxury, a **meretricious** taste in the splendor.
>
> —Honoré de Balzac
> *Old Goriot* (1835)

206. meticulous

adjective

Taking extreme care with minute details; precise; thorough.

> Moreover, in his tremendous prophecy of this kingdom which was to make all men one together in God, Jesus had small patience for the bargaining righteousness of formal religion. Another large part of his recorded utterances is aimed against the **meticulous** observance of the rules of the pious career.
>
> —H. G. Wells
> *A Short History of the World* (1922)

207. mettle

noun

Courage or fortitude; also temperament or disposition, as in *a woman of fine mettle.*

> In truth, the Geats' prince gladly trusted
> his **mettle**, his might, the mercy of God!
> Cast off then his corselet of iron,
> helmet from head; to his henchman gave,—
> choicest of weapons,—the well-chased sword,
> bidding him guard the gear of battle.
>
> —*Beowulf*
>
> Translated by Francis B. Gummere (1910)

208. microcosm

noun

A small representative system analogous to the larger system.

> Thus one can see in the Negro church to-day, reproduced in **microcosm**, all that great world from which the Negro is cut off by color-prejudice and social condition. In the great city churches the same tendency is noticeable and in many respects emphasized. A great church like the Bethel of Philadelphia has over eleven hundred members, an edifice seating fifteen hundred persons and valued at one hundred thousand dollars, an annual budget of five thousand dollars, and a government consisting of a pastor with several assisting local preachers, an executive and legislative board, financial boards and tax collectors; general church meetings for making laws; subdivided groups led by class leaders, a

> company of militia, and twenty-four auxiliary societies.
>
> —W. E. B. Du Bois
> *The Souls of Black Folk* (1903)

209. mien

noun

Air, demeanor, or bearing, which shows feeling or character.

> My Lord advances with majestic **mien**,
> Smit with the mighty pleasure to be seen.
>
> —Alexander Pope
> *Moral Essays: Epistle to Richard Boyle, Earl of Burlington* (1731)

210. militate, mitigate

verb

Militate: to influence strongly. The word *militate* is intransitive and is usually accompanied by the preposition *against*.

> For if it happened that an individual, even when asleep, had some very distinct idea, as, for example, if a geometer should discover some new demonstration, the circumstance of his being asleep would not **militate** against its truth.
>
> —René Descartes
> *Discourse on Method* (1637)

Mitigate: to make less severe or less intense. The word *mitigate* is transitive and may affix itself directly to a noun.

> The joys of parents are secret; and so are their griefs and fears. They cannot utter the one; nor they will not utter the other. Children sweeten labors; but they make misfortunes more bitter. They increase the cares of life; but they **mitigate** the remembrance of death. The perpetuity by generation is common to beasts; but memory, merit, and noble works are proper to men.
>
> —Francis Bacon
> *Essays, Civil and Moral* (1909)

211. misanthropic

adjective

Characterized by a mistrustful scorn or hatred of humankind; having a sneering disbelief in humankind.

Note: The noun *misanthrope* (a person) is a hater of humankind. The noun *misanthropy* refers to the hatred itself.

> Wilhelm checked his feelings: Jarno's extravagant, untimely laughter had in truth offended him. "It is scarcely hiding your **misanthropy**," said he, "when you maintain that faults like these are universal."
>
> —J. W. von Goethe
> *Wilhelm Meister's Apprenticeship* (1873)

212. misnomer

noun

A name wrongly or mistakenly applied; an inappropriate or misapplied designation or name.

> Cat-nap is a short nap taken while sitting; cat-ladder a kind of ladder used on sloping roofs of houses; cat-steps, the projections of the stones in the slanting part of the gable; cat-pipe, an artificial cat-call. Puss gentleman is eighteenth century for catamite. Kitty is a common poker term. Copy cat is a **misnomer** because cats never copy anybody. A common phrase for an unusual event is "enough to make a cat laugh," but the Cheshire Cat in "Alice in Wonderland" is not the only recorded example of a laughing cat. "Enough to make a cat speak" is a similar expression, but as I have pointed out in the preceding chapter, speaking cats are almost a commonplace.
>
> —Carl Van Vechten
> *The Tiger in the House* (1922)

213. missive

noun

A message in writing; a letter.

> George read one sentence in this letter several times. Then he dropped the **missive** in his wastebasket to join the clipping, and strolled down the corridor of his dormitory to borrow a copy of "Twelfth Night." Having

> secured one, he returned to his study and refreshed his memory of the play—but received no enlightenment that enabled him to comprehend Lucy's strange remark. However, he found himself impelled in the direction of correspondence, and presently wrote a letter—not a reply to his Aunt Fanny.
>
> —Booth Tarkington
> *The Magnificent Ambersons* (1918)

214. mitigate, militate

See the discussion under *militate, mitigate.*

215. moribund

adjective

About to die; on the verge of termination or extinction; on the verge of becoming obsolete.

> Of the twenty or so civilizations known to modern Western historians, all except our own appear to be dead or **moribund**, and, when we diagnose each case, *in extremis* or *post mortem,* we invariably find that the cause of death has been either War or Class or some combination of the two.
>
> —Arnold J. Toynbee
> *Civilization on Trial* (1948)

216. munificent

adjective

Characterized by generous motives, extremely liberal in giving.

Yesterday was a big moment in the annals of congressional **munificence**. While the Senate was increasing the government's borrowing limit and growing the budget, the House was having a little Vote-a-Rama of its own, adding goodies to a $92 billion spending package to pay for Iraq and hurricane recovery.

—Dana Milbank
"Welcome to Spend City"
Washington Post, March 17, 2006

217. myriad

noun

A vast indefinite number.

adjective

Innumerable.

Note: Throughout most of its history in English *myriad* was used as a noun, as in *a myriad of men.* In the 19th century it began to be used in poetry as an adjective, as in *myriad men.* Both usages in English are acceptable, as in Samuel Taylor Coleridge's "Myriad myriads of lives." This poetic, adjectival use became so well entrenched generally that many people came to consider it as the only correct use. In fact, both uses in English are parallel with those of the original ancient Greek. The Greek word *mûrias*, from which *myriad* derives, could be used as either a noun or an adjective, but the noun *mûrias* was used in general prose and in mathematics while the adjective *mûrias* was used only in poetry.

—Dictionary.reference.com/
browse/myriad

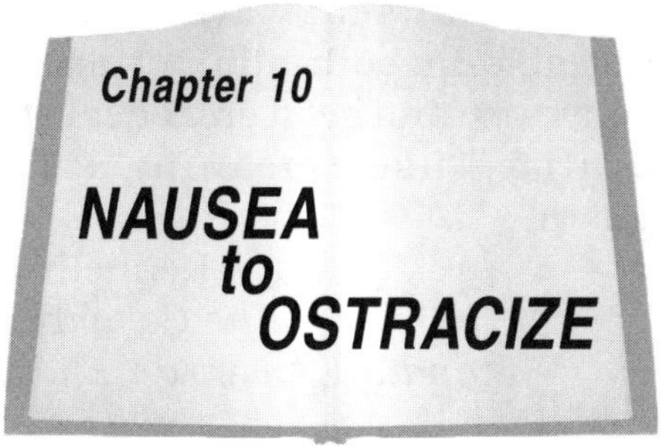

218. nausea, nauseate, nauseous, nauseating

nausea, noun; *nauseate*, verb; *nauseous*, *nauseated*, and *nauseating*, adjectives.

Note: Purists insist that *nauseous* means "causing nausea," as in *the nauseous roller-coaster ride*, and that *nauseated* means "feeling nausea," as in *the nauseated student rushed from the room*. But these days, both adjectives have both meanings. In formal writing, however, it's best to observe the distinctions. Consider the following:

> The problem is whether *nauseous* can be restricted to meaning "causing nausea" and *nauseated* to meaning "feeling nausea," which orderly division is what most Edited English tries to enforce. But alas for neatness, both adjectives have both meanings, though a few dictionaries insist that *nauseous,* meaning "feeling nausea," is limited to Colloquial use. Best advice: follow the Edited English practice in speech and writing, and no one will object. In adjunct use *nauseous* and *nauseating,* meaning

> "causing nausea," are roughly interchangeable in both adjunct and predicate adjective use and get a great deal of Standard figurative use meaning "sickening, disgusting."
>
> —Kenneth G. Wilson
> *The Columbia Guide to Standard American English* (1993)

219. nefarious

adjective

Wicked or villainous in the extreme; vile, heinous.

> One of the most **nefarious** aspects of the court of Constantinople (known as the Seraglio and the Sublime Porte) was the all-pervading corruption and bribery that had been raised to a system of administration. The pashas and hospodars (governors) who administered the provinces and vassal states purchased their posts at exorbitant prices. They recovered their fortunes by extorting still larger sums from their subjects. The peasantry was thus reduced to abject misery.
>
> —"Ottoman Empire"
> *The Columbia Encyclopedia*, 6th ed. (2001–07)

220. nihilism, nihilist

noun

Nihilism: the total rejection of laws and institutions; *nihilism* is marked by terrorism, anarchy, and other revolutionary activity. In philosophy, *nihilism* is an extreme form of skepticism, the denial of all existence or the possibility of an objective basis for truth.

noun

Nihilist: an advocate of *nihilism.*

> But in conversations along the streets of Jordan's 10 camps, the Palestinians tell a story, however anecdotal, of a landscape where secular politics has withered, Islamic activism is ascendant and, perhaps more important, a sense of dejection, even **nihilism**, is rising, with uncertain consequences.
>
> —Anthony Shadid
> "In Jordanian Camps,
> A Sense of **Nihilism**"
> *Washington Post*, April 7, 2007

221. noisome, noisy

adjective

Noisome: very offensive, particularly to the sense of smell, as in *noisome fumes*.

Noisy: loud.

Note: The human ear can detect only one of these words, that is, *noisy*. The other, *noisome*, is better associated with the nose.

> Foul words is but foul wind, and foul wind is but foul breath, and foul breath is **noisome**; therefore I will depart unkissed.
>
> —William Shakespeare
> *Much Ado about Nothing* (1598–99)

222. nonpareil

noun, adjective

A person or thing without equal, peerless; a small pellet of sugar used for decorating cookies or candy; a bite-sized chocolate covered with these pellets.

> I see you what you are: you are too proud;
> But, if you were the devil, you are fair.
> My lord and master loves you: O! such love
> Could be but recompensed, though you were crowned
> The **nonpareil** of beauty.
>
> —William Shakespeare
> *Twelfth Night* (1601)

223. nostrum

noun

A medicine sold with exaggerated claims of its efficacy; quack medicine; snake oil; a scheme, theory, or device, especially one to remedy social or political ills.

> As to Squire Western, he was seldom out of the sickroom, unless when he was engaged either in the field or over his bottle. Nay, he would sometimes retire hither to take his beer, and it was not without difficulty that

> he was prevented from forcing Jones to take his beer too: for no quack ever held his **nostrum** to be a more general panacea than he did this; which, he said, had more virtue in it than was in all the physic in an apothecary's shop.
>
> —Henry Fielding
> *The History of Tom Jones* (1749)

224. nuance

noun

A slight degree of difference in anything perceptible; a very slight variation or difference in color or tone.

> Throughout these eight or ten volumes he proves himself to be one of those rare writers who see what they write. As in the case of Tennyson, than whom no English poet, in spite of nearsightedness, has observed so minutely the tiniest details of form or the faintest **nuance** of color, so the lack of normal vision did not prevent Roosevelt from being the closest of observers. He was also, by the way, a good shot with rifle or pistol.
>
> —William Roscoe Thayer
> *Theodore Roosevelt* (1919)

225. obdurate

adjective

Unmoved by pity, persuasion, or tender feelings; stubborn, unyielding; resistant to moral influence.

> She stood with her bright angry eyes confronting the wide stare, and the set face;

> and softened no more, when the moaning was repeated, than if the face had been a picture.
>
> "Miss Dartle," said I, "if you can be so **obdurate** as not to feel for this afflicted mother—"
>
> "Who feels for me?" she sharply retorted. "She has sown this. Let her moan for the harvest that she reaps to-day!"
>
> —Charles Dickens
> *David Copperfield* (1850)

226. obsequious

adjective

Showing a servile or fawning readiness to fall in with the wishes or will of another; overly deferential.

> What guest at Dives's table can pass the familiar house without a sigh?—the familiar house of which the lights used to shine so cheerfully at seven o'clock, of which the hall-doors opened so readily, of which the **obsequious** servants, as you passed up the comfortable stair, sounded your name from landing to landing, until it reached the apartment where jolly old Dives welcomed his friends! What a number of them he had; and what a noble way of entertaining them. How witty people used to be here who were morose when they got out of the door; and how courteous and friendly men who slandered and hated each other everywhere else! He was pompous, but with such a cook what would one not swallow? He was rather

dull, perhaps, but would not such wine make any conversation pleasant?

—William M. Thackeray
Vanity Fair (1847–48)

227. obstinate

adjective

Stubbornly or firmly adhering to one's own view, purpose, or opinion; unyielding in attitude; inflexible persistence, as in *obstinate advocacy for higher taxes*; not easily controlled, as in *obstinate growth of weeds.* There are also many other Cubans who have dreamed for years of Fidel's demise, convinced that fate has dealt them a heavy hand by turning over their lives to this particularly **obstinate**, egocentric and durable man. Under Fidel, their lives have been spent in a kind of suffocating reality warp, a uniquely Cuban realm in which time simultaneously stands still and progresses, see-sawing among dramatic episodes linked inextricably to Fidel's whim and will.

—Jon Lee Anderson
"Fidel's Slow Fade"
Los Angeles Times, February 20, 2008

228. obstreperous

adjective

Resisting restraint or control in a difficult manner; unruly; boistrous, noisy, clamorous.

A lunatic may be "soothed,"... for a time, but in the end, he is very apt to become

> **obstreperous**. His cunning, too, is proverbial, and great.... When a madman appears thoroughly sane, indeed, it is high time to put him in a straight jacket.
>
> —Edgar Allan Poe
> "The System of Doctor Tarr and Professor Fether"
> *Graham's Magazine* (1845)

229. obtuse

adjective

Not alert or quick in perception or feeling; dull; not observant; not sharp or pointed, blunt in form.

> It is because the public are a mass—inert, **obtuse**, and passive—that they need to be shaken up from time to time so that we can tell from their bear-like grunts where they are—and also where they stand. They are pretty harmless, in spite of their numbers, because they are fighting against intelligence.
>
> —Alfred Jarry
> "Theater Questions"
> *La Revue Blanche* (1897)
> Reprinted in
> *The Selected Works of Alfred Jarry* (1965)

230. obviate

verb

To anticipate, eliminate, or prevent difficulties by effective measures, as in *to obviate the risk of injury.*

> The Internet, on the other hand, not only creates niche communities—of young people, beer aficionados, news junkies, Britney Spears fanatics—that seem to **obviate** the need for the larger community, it plays to another powerful force in modern America and one that also undermines the movies: narcissism.
>
> —Neal Gabler
> "The Movie Magic Is Gone"
> *Los Angeles Times*, February 25, 2007

231. officious

adjective

Intermeddling with what is not one's concern; overly aggressive in offering one's unwanted and unrequested services.

> The government is huge, stupid, greedy and makes nosy, **officious** and dangerous intrusions into the smallest corners of life—this much we can stand. But the real problem is that government is boring. We could cure or mitigate the other ills Washington visits on us if we could only bring ourselves to pay attention to Washington itself. But we cannot.
>
> —P. J. O'Rourke
> "The Mystery of Government"
> *Parliament of Whores* (1991)

232. omniscience, omniscient

adjective

Omniscient: having unlimited or infinite knowledge.

noun

Omniscience: unlimited or infinite knowledge.

> Philip felt that he ought to have been thoroughly happy in that answer of hers; she was as open and transparent as a rock-pool. Why was he not thoroughly happy? Jealousy is never satisfied with anything short of an **omniscience** that would detect the subtlest fold of the heart.
>
> —George Eliot
> *The Mill on the Floss* (1860)

233. onerous

adjective

Burdensome, oppressive, troublesome.

> We have the means to change the laws we find unjust or **onerous**. We cannot, as citizens, pick and choose the laws we will or will not obey.
>
> —Former President Ronald Reagan
> Speech to the United Brotherhood of Carpenters and Joiners after he dismissed 12,000 air traffic controllers who went out on a strike in violation of federal law
> Chicago, Illinois, September 3, 1981

234. onus

noun

A difficult burden, task, or responsibility. In law, the word *onus* refers to the burden of proof, as in *The onus is on the plaintiff to prove negligence.*

> He proposed to call witnesses to show how the prisoner, a profligate and spendthrift, had been at the end of his financial tether, and had also been carrying on an intrigue with a certain Mrs. Raikes, a neighbouring farmer's wife. This having come to his stepmother's ears, she taxed him with it on the afternoon before her death, and a quarrel ensued, part of which was overheard. On the previous day, the prisoner had purchased strychnine at the village chemist's shop, wearing a disguise by means of which he hoped to throw the **onus** of the crime upon another man—to wit, Mrs. Inglethorp's husband, of whom he had been bitterly jealous. Luckily for Mr. Inglethorp, he had been able to produce an unimpeachable alibi.
>
> —Agatha Christie
> *The Mysterious Affair at Styles* (1924)

235. opprobrium

noun

The disgrace or reproach incurred by outrageous or shameful conduct; ignominy.

> Yahoo has suffered a good deal of **opprobrium** since it was revealed last month that, when [Chinese] government officials came calling, the company's Hong Kong division simply surrendered information on

a Chinese citizen who had presumably sought refuge, anonymity and a bit of freedom in the bosom of a Yahoo e-mail address.

—Tom Zeller Jr.
"Yahoo in China: Rising Tide of Anger"
International Herald Tribune,
October 24, 2005

236. oral, verbal

adjective

Oral: uttered by the mouth, as in *oral testimony*; using or transmitted by speech, as in *oral methods of teaching languages*; involving the mouth, as in *the oral cavity*; taken, done, or administered through the mouth, as in *an oral dose of medicine*. *Verbal*: pertaining to words, as in *verbal ability*; in the form of words, as in *verbal images*; expressed in spoken words, as in *verbal agreement*.

Note: Many insist that *oral* relates to spoken words and that *verbal* does not mean *oral*. But *verbal* has meant *oral* since the sixteenth century.

Verbal has had the meaning "spoken" since the late 16th century and is thus synonymous with *oral*: *He wrote a memorandum to confirm the verbal agreement*. Slightly earlier, *verbal* had developed the meaning "expressed in words, whether spoken or written (as opposed to actions)": *Verbal support is no help without money and supplies*. Although some say that the use of *verbal* to mean "spoken" produces ambiguity, it rarely does so. *Verbal* is used in this sense in all varieties of speech and writing and is fully standard. The context usually makes the meaning clear: *No documents are necessary; a verbal agreement* (or *contract* or *order*) *will suffice.* Oral can be used instead of *verbal* if the context demands: *My lawyer insists on a written contract because oral agreements are too difficult to enforce.*

—Dictionary.reference.com/
browse/verbal

237. ostracize

verb

To exclude, by general agreement, from friendship, society, conversation, or privileges, as in *His friends ostracized him after the scandal broke.*

> Even after this skirmish, Democrats are unlikely to completely **ostracize** Fox [New Channel]. John Edwards, who was the first to withdraw from the Nevada debate, said this week he wouldn't preclude future appearances on the network. And insiders say that despite another online uproar, the Congressional Black Caucus intends next week to announce plans to co-sponsor a Democratic presidential debate with Fox, just as it did in 2004.
>
> —Ronald Brownstein
> "Fox Hounded: How the Democrats
> Are Turning on Fox News"
> *Los Angeles Times*, March 16, 2007

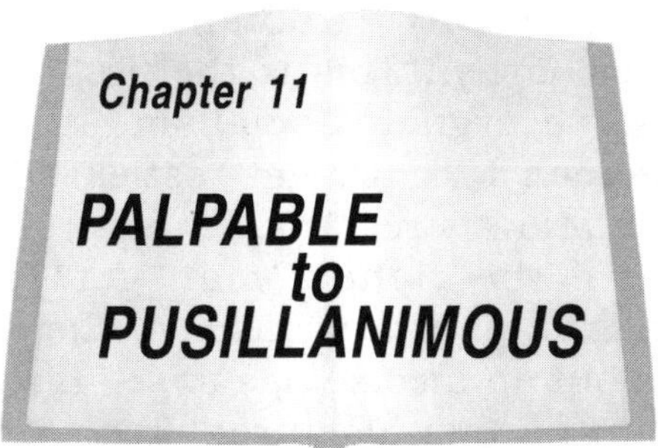

238. palpable

noun

Plainly or readily seen, heard, or understood; evident; obvious; capable of being felt or touched; tangible.

> Is this a dagger which I see before me,
> The handle toward my hand? Come, let me clutch thee.
> I have thee not, and yet I see thee still.
> Art thou not, fatal vision, sensible
> To feeling as to sight? or art thou but
> A dagger of the mind, a false creation,
> Proceeding from the heat-oppressed brain?
> I see thee yet, in form as **palpable**
> As this which now I draw.
>
> —William Shakespeare
> *Macbeth*

239. panacea

noun

A remedy or medicine for all disease, a cure-all; a solution for all difficulties or problems.

"It's not all rubbish," cried Amory passionately. "This is the first time in my life I've argued Socialism. It's the only **panacea** I know. I'm restless. My whole generation is restless. I'm sick of a system where the richest man gets the most beautiful girl if he wants her, where the artist without an income has to sell his talents to a button manufacturer. Even if I had no talents I'd not be content to work ten years, condemned either to celibacy or a furtive indulgence, to give some man's son an automobile."

—F. Scott Fitzgerald
This Side of Paradise (1920)

240. pandemic

adjective, noun

Affecting a whole people, all classes, or the whole world, as a disease; general or universal, as in *pandemic fear of terrorist attacks.*

"The threat of an influenza **pandemic** is, at present, one of the most significant public health issues our nation and world faces."

—Dr. Andrew C. von Eschenback
Commissioner of the U.S. Food
and Drug Administration, April 2007

"We know that a **pandemic** will eventually occur. We always say it's not a question of if; it's a question of when."

—Dr. Julie Gerberding
Director of the Centers for Disease
Control and Prevention, April 2007

241. parable

noun

A brief story used to teach a truth or moral lesson; a statement or comment that conveys an indirect meaning through analogy or comparison.

> He put before them another **parable**: "The kingdom of heaven is like a mustard seed that someone took and sowed in his field; it is the smallest of all the seeds, but when it has grown it is the greatest of shrubs and becomes a tree, so that the birds of the air come and make nests in its branches."
>
> —Matthew 13:31–32
> New Testament

242. paradigm

noun

A pattern or model; a set of assumptions, values, concepts, and practices that forms a way of viewing reality for the people who share those assumptions, etc., especially in an intellectual discipline.

> Manhattanism is the one urbanistic ideology that has fed, from its conception, on the splendors and miseries of the metropolitan condition—hyper-density—without once losing faith in it as the basis for a desirable modern culture. Manhattan's architecture is a **paradigm** for the exploitation of congestion.
>
> —Rem Koolhaas
> *Delirious New York* (1978)

243. paragon

noun

A pattern or model of excellence.

> Based on the novel by Charles Baxter, the movie is ostensibly an exploration of love in its many forms, but mostly it sticks to the credulity-and-patience-straining kind. Morgan Freeman, cast again as a **paragon** of perfection (just once, it would be great to see him play a spiteful neurotic or a selfish bastard), plays Harry Stevenson, a happily married university professor who, when not at home regaling his loving wife, Esther (Jane Alexander), with stories about youngsters falling in love before his very eyes, hangs out in a local cafe dispensing gems.
>
> —Carina Chocano
> Film Review of *Feast of Love* (2007)
> *Los Angeles Times*, September 28, 2007

244. parlance

noun

A manner or way of speaking, vernacular, idiom, as in *legal parlance.*

> Every president after Jefferson has professed agreement with Jefferson's concept that the freedom of the American press to print its versions of the facts, background and likely consequences of human events was a constitutional principle permanently reserved from any form of interference by

government. Consequently Jefferson denounced ... either direct or indirect attempts by government to do what in current **parlance** has become known as "management of the news."

—Arthur Krock
"Mr. Kennedy's Management of the News"
Fortune, March 1963

245. parody

verb

A satirical or humorous imitation, usually of a serious piece of literature; any humorous, burlesque, or satirical imitation of a person, event, etc.

The **parody** is the last refuge of the frustrated writer. **Parodies** are what you write when you are associate editor of the *Harvard Lampoon*. The greater the work of literature, the easier the **parody**. The step up from writing **parodies** is writing on the wall above the urinal.

—Ernest Hemingway
Quoted in *Papa Hemingway*
by A.E. Hotchner (1966)

246. parsimonious

adjective

Unduly sparing in the use or expenditure of money; stingy; cheap.

England, however, as it has never been

> blessed with a very **parsimonious** government, so **parsimony** has at no time been the characteristical virtue of its inhabitants. It is the highest impertinence and presumption, therefore, in kings and ministers to pretend to watch over the economy of private people, and to restrain their expence, either by sumptuary laws, or by prohibiting the importation of foreign luxuries. They are themselves always, and without any exception, the greatest spendthrifts in the society. Let them look well after their own expence, and they may safely trust private people with theirs. If their own extravagance does not ruin the state, that of their subjects never will.
>
> —Adam Smith
> *Wealth of Nations* (1776)

247. patronize

verb

To give a store or business one's regular patronage; to trade with; to behave in an offensively condescending way.

> "Of course," his mother persevered, "some of the programs are not very good, but we ought to **patronize** them and make the best of what we have."
>
> —Willa Cather
> *One of Ours* (1922)

> A rather fast crowd had come out, who drank cocktails in limousines and were promiscuously condescending and

> **patronizing** toward older people, and Eleanor with an esprit that hinted strongly of the boulevards, led many innocents still redolent of St. Timothy's and Farmington, into paths of Bohemian naughtiness.
>
> —F. Scott Fitzgerald
> *This Side of Paradise* (1920)

248. paucity

noun

Smallness of quantity; scarcity.

> It is very strange, and very melancholy, that the **paucity** of human pleasures should persuade us ever to call hunting one of them.
>
> —Samuel Johnson
> *Anecdotes of Samuel Johnson* (1786)

249. pecuniary

adjective

Of or relating to money.

> No genuine equality, no real freedom, no true manhood or womanhood can exist on any foundation save that of **pecuniary** independence. As a right over a man's subsistence is a power over his moral being, so a right over a woman's subsistence enslaves her will, degrades her pride and vitiates her whole moral nature.
>
> —Susan B. Anthony
> Quoted in *The Life of Susan B. Anthony* by Ida Husted Harper (1897)

250. pedagogy

noun

The science and art of teaching; the function or work of a teacher.

> The first thing to know about Lan Samantha Chang, who has been named the new director of the Iowa Writers' Workshop, is that she has strong ideas about teaching.
>
> —Dinitia Smith
> "For Writers' Program, a New **Pedagogy**"
> *New York Times,* April 18, 2005

251. pedantic

adjective

Ostentatious in one's learning; characterized by a detailed, often ostentatious, attention to formalisms, especially in teaching.

> Here, Nabokov's aristocratic dilettantism is perfect, because he uses it to flick off the Bolsheviks as if *they* were nothing more than clumsy servants—overzealous, **pedantic**, too eager. This is moving because we learn, three words after "**pedantic**" where their **pedantry** ended up: They shot Osip dead. And this word gains an extra strength from our sense that Nabokov is himself being **pedantic** at this moment. He is being **pedantic** for insisting on using the word "**pedantic**"! His very precision of language is deliciously **pedantic**. And so Nabokov's sympathetic **pedantry** vanquishes the murderous **pedantry** of the Bolsheviks, and, in the

> space of this sentence, art does truly triumph over history, and style over content.
>
> —James Wood
> "Discussing Nabokov: Delicious **Pedantry**"
> *Slate.com*, April 26, 1999

252. pejorative

adjective

Characterized by a belittling, disparaging, or derogatory force or effect.

noun

The statement itself.

> Never . . . use the word *gossip* in a **pejorative** sense. It's the very stuff of biography and has to be woven in. To suggest that the personal life is not an essential element in the creative life is absurd.
>
> —Joan Peyser
> *Publishers Weekly*, June 5, 1987

253. penultimate

adjective

Next to the last.

> When I was a school-boy, during the **penultimate** decade of the last century, the chief American grammar was "A Practical Grammar of the English Language," by Thomas W. Harvey. This formidable work was almost purely synthetical: it began with

> a long series of definitions, wholly unintelligible to a child, and proceeded into a maddening maze of pedagogical distinctions, puzzling even to an adult.
>
> —H. L. Mencken
> *The American Language* (1921)

254. penurious

adjective

Excessively sparing in the use of money; extremely stingy; extremely poor or destitute.

> These new "malefactors of great wealth" are not just distant figures hurrying toward their private jets bound for some purchased paradise; no, in many cases they have been entrusted with the pension funds of millions of Americans who are faced with the prospect of a **penurious** old age.
>
> —Mary McGrory
> "Changing the Subject"
> *Washington Post*, July 7, 2002

255. pernicious

adjective

Causing serious ruin or harm; injurious; deadly.

> The machine has had a **pernicious** effect upon virtue, pity, and love, and young men used to machines which induce inertia, and fear, are near impotents.
>
> —Edward Dahlberg
> "No Love and No Thanks"
> *Alms for Oblivion* (1964)

256. perquisite

noun

A payment, advantage, benefit, or privilege received beyond regular income or salary; something claimed as an exclusive right.

Note: The expression "perk" comes from *perquisite.*

> Assassination is the **perquisite** of princes.
> —A nineteenth-century cliché in European courts

257. perspicacious, perspicacity

adjective

Perspicacious: having a keen mental understanding or perception; shrewd; astute; discerning.

noun

Perspicacity: keen mental understanding or perception; shrewdness; astuteness.

Note: Do not confuse *perspicacious* with *perspicuous* or *perspicacity* with *perspicuity.* Consider the following discussion:

> If you display ***perspicacious*** qualities, you appear to have good judgment; you are perceptive, and therefore you have ***perspicacity***. If you display ***perspicuous*** qualities, you are clear of statement, lucid; you make things clear, and hence you have ***perspicuity***. These relatively low frequency pairs may be hard to keep distinct, but there

> are those who will fault you for confusing them: look them up rather than risk using them inaccurately, or choose instead some words you understand.
>
> —Kenneth G. Wilson
> *The Columbia Guide to Standard American English* (1993)

258. perusal, peruse

noun

Perusal: the act of reading carefully or thoughtfully; scrutiny; survey.

verb

Peruse: to read thoroughly and carefully; to examine or survey in detail.

> Call it the Pulitzer Early Warning System. In **perusing** the list of well-achieved journalistic Pulitzers today, one fact cried out: all the major national news reporting awards went to big national media. *The Washington Post* won 4 and the *New York Times* won 3, testimony to importance of their continuing investment in investigative reporting in the national interest.
>
> What the Pulitzers Tell Us About Newspaper Fortunes
> April 18, 2006
> —Contentbridges.com/2006/04/what_the_pulitz.html

259. petulant

adjective

Showing sudden or impatient irritation, especially over something trifling; irritable, peevish, fretful, petty.

> The faces of most American women over thirty are relief maps of **petulant** and bewildered unhappiness.
>
> —F. Scott Fitzgerald
> Letter to his daughter, Frances Scott Fitzgerald, October 5, 1940

260. phlegmatic

adjective

Not easily roused to feeling, emotion, or action; composed, calm, self-possessed; having a sluggish, unemotional temperament.

> **Phlegmatic** natures can be inspired to enthusiasm only by being made into fanatics.
>
> —Friedrich Nietzsche
> *Sämtliche Werke: Kritische Studienausgabe* (1980)

261. pique

verb

To excite a degree of anger and resentment, as in *She was piqued by their refusal to attend the party*; to excite interest or curiosity in; to arouse or provoke to action.

> "It naturally happens this time of year that people get interested in IRAs, but [the pension legislation] certainly has **piqued**

> people's interest," says Catherine Gordon, a principal at Vanguard Group.
>
> —Jilian Mincer
> "Pension Act May **Pique** Interest in IRAs"
> *Wall Street Journal*, February 6, 2007

Note: As a noun, *pique* denotes a feeling of irritation or resentment.

> This dog and man at first were friends;
> But when a **pique** began,
> The dog, to gain some private ends,
> Went mad and bit the man.
>
> —Oliver Goldsmith

262. plebeian

adjective

Commonplace, vulgar or coarse in nature; of or associated with the great masses of people; relating to or belonging to the ancient Roman plebs.

noun

A member of the common people; also a member of the ancient Roman plebs.

> The modern picture of The Artist began to form: The poor, but free spirit, **plebeian** but aspiring only to be classless, to cut himself forever free from the bonds of the greedy bourgeoisie, to be whatever the fat burghers feared most, to cross the line wherever they drew it, to look at the world in a way they couldn't see, to be high, live low, stay young forever—in short, to be the bohemian.
>
> —Tom Wolfe
> *The Painted Word* (1975)

263. poignant

adjective

Profoundly touching or moving; strong in mental appeal; affecting the emotions.

> There are few sorrows, however **poignant**, in which a good income is of no avail.
>
> —Logan Pearsall Smith
> "Life and Human Nature"
> *Afterthoughts* (1931)

264. portend

verb

To indicate in advance, especially by previous signs; to presage, foreshadow; to signify, mean.

> "Rise in Cases of West Nile May **Portend** an Epidemic"
>
> —Denise Grady
> *New York Times* Headline
> July 26, 2007

265. portent

noun

Anything that indicates what is about to happen; a significant threat; a marvel or prodigy, something amazing.

> Self-parody is the first **portent** of age.
>
> —Larry McMurtry
> *Some Can Whistle* (1989)

266. precarious

adjective

Dependent on circumstances beyond one's control; lacking in stability or security; subject to change; based on unproved premises; perilous.

> A politician never forgets the **precarious** nature of elective life. We have never established a practice of tenure in public office.
>
> —Hubert H. Humphrey
> Speech at the University of Wisconsin,
> August 23, 1965

267. precedence, precedent, precedential

noun

Precedence: the fact or act of preceding, as in *The first patent application receives precedence in Europe*; priority in place, time, or rank because of superiority, as in *The company relied on its precedence as the leading producer of computer chips*; a ceremonial rank or preference.

Precedent: in law, a judicial or other legal decision that establishes a rule to be followed by lower courts or tribunals; any decision or act that serves as a guide.
adjective

Precedential: having precedence, usually because of longer service; having the character of a precedent or guide.

> The man who will follow **precedent**, but never create one, is merely an obvious example of the routineer [a person who follows routine]. You find him desperately numerous in the civil service, in the official bureaus. To him government is something given as unconditionally, as absolutely as ocean or hill. He goes on winding the tape that he finds. His imagination has rarely extricated itself from under the administrative machine to gain any sense of what a human, temporary contraption the whole affair is. What he thinks is the heavens above him is nothing but the roof.
>
> —Walter Lippmann
> *A Preface to Politics* (1913)

268. preclude

verb

To prevent the occurrence or existence of something; to exclude from something.

> Anyone who has breast-fed knows two things for sure: The baby wants to be fed at the most inopportune times, in the most inopportune places, and the baby will prevail. . . . And so the baby should, and the mom, too. Sometimes a breast is a sexual object, and sometimes it's a food delivery system, and one need not **preclude** nor color the other.
>
> —Anna Quindlen
> "Public & Private: To Feed or Not to Feed"
> *New York Times*, May 25, 1994

269. precocious

adjective

Unusually mature or advanced in development, especially in mental aptitude; usually in reference to children.

> What might be taken for a **precocious** genius is the genius of childhood. When the child grows up, it disappears without a trace. It may happen that this boy will become a real painter some day, or even a great painter. But then he will have to begin everything again, from zero.
>
> —Pablo Picasso
> Quoted in *Picasso and Company*
> by Gyula Brassaï (1966)

270. precursor

noun

A person or thing that precedes; a person, animal, or thing indicating the approach of something or someone, a harbinger.

> In his very rejection of art Walt Whitman is an artist. He tried to produce a certain effect by certain means and he succeeded. . . . He stands apart, and the chief value of his work is in its prophecy, not in its performance. He has begun a prelude to larger themes. He is the herald to a new era. As a man he is the **precursor** of a fresh type. He is a factor in the heroic and spiritual evolution of the human being. If Poetry has passed him by,

> Philosophy will take note of him.
>
> —Oscar Wilde
> Review of *November Boughs*
> by Walt Whitman
> *Pall Mall Gazette*, January 25, 1889

271. predilection

noun

A tendency or inclination to think favorably about something, a preference, as in *a predilection for Mozart.*

> The parrot holds its food for prim consumption as daintily as any debutante, [with] a **predilection** for pot roast, hashed-brown potatoes, duck skin, butter, hoisin sauce, sesame seed oil, bananas and human thumb.
>
> —Alexander Theroux
> "I Sing the Parrot!"
> *Reader's Digest*, May 1983

272. premise

noun

A proposition on which an argument is based or from which a conclusion is drawn. In law, *premises* refers to land and buildings on the land.
verb

To assume or state as a proposition in an argument.

> The utopian male concept which is the **premise** of male pornography is this—since

> manhood is established and confirmed over and against the brutalized bodies of women, men need not aggress against each other; in other words, women absorb male aggression so that men are safe from it.
>
> —Andrea Dworkin
> Speech at Massachusetts Institute of Technology, September 26, 1975
> "The Root Cause"
> *Our Blood* (1976)

273. prerogative

noun

Exclusive privilege or right, obtained or exercised because of rank or office, as in *prerogatives of a member of Congress.*

> Elegance is not the **prerogative** of those who have just escaped from adolescence, but of those who have already taken possession of their future.
>
> —Gabrielle "Coco" Chanel
> *McCall's*, November 1965

274. prescience, prescient

noun

Prescience: knowledge of events before they take place.
adjective

Prescient: perceiving significance of events before they take place.

***Note*:** The first syllable is pronounced either *pree-* or *presh-*.

> He said, I'm just out of hospital,
> but I'm still flying.
> I answered, of course,
> angry, **prescient**, knowing.
> what fire lay behind his wide stare . . . .
>
> —Hilda Doolittle
> "R.A.F . . ."

275. presumption, presumptuous

noun

Presumption: that which may be logically assumed to be true until disproved; an assumption. In law, a fact assumed because of the proof of other facts; in patent law, for example, a patent enjoys a "presumption of validity" because it was issued by the U.S. Patent and Trademark Office; in a lawsuit for patent infringement, however, the alleged infringer will seek to show that the patent is not valid, for a variety of reasons.

adjective

Presumptuous, impertinent, unjustifiably bold, excessively forward.

***Note*:** The adjective *presumptive* means having a reasonable basis for acceptance or belief, as in *the presumptive candidate for president.*

> You may consider me **presumptuous**, gentlemen, but I claim to be a citizen of the United States, with all the qualifications of a voter. I can read the Constitution, I am

> possessed of two hundred and fifty dollars, and the last time I looked in the old family Bible I found I was over twenty-one years of age.
>
> —Elizabeth Cady Stanton
> Quoted in *History of Woman Suffrage* (1881)

276. prevaricate

verb

To use ambiguous or evasive language for the purpose of deceiving or diverting attention; to tell a falsehood; to lie.

> Lying is the same as alcoholism. Liars **prevaricate** even on their deathbeds.
>
> —Anton Pavlovich Chekhov
> Letter to the writer A.N. Pleshcheev, October 9, 1888
> "Nauka," *Complete Works and Letters in Thirty Volumes* (1976)

277. principal, principle

noun

Principal: the head of a school; also means "money" or "the balance on your mortgage." As an adjective, ***principal*** means "main."

Principle: acts only as a noun. It means "rule" or "moral tenet."

Use this trick:
A principal should be your **pal. Principle** ends in **-le**. So does **rule**.

Example: According to the **principal** rule at Sunshine Elementary, you must obey the **principal** and respect the **principles** of democracy.

278. privity, privy

noun

Privity: knowledge shared with another or others regarding a private matter. In law, a relationship between or among parties, typically to a contract.

Privy: an outhouse; a person having an interest in a legal transaction or legal relationship. As an adjective, participating in the knowledge of something private, usually followed by *to*, as in *We are privy to his plan.*

Note on the law: Historically, *privity* between the parties was required for tort liability to exist. So if Joe buys a defective car and sells it to Pete and Pete is injured, Pete could not sue the manufacturer that sold the car to Joe. Today, however, subsequent purchasers, who were obviously not *privies* to the original contract first signed years ago, may sue, despite the lack of *privity*. Warranty statutes and strict products liability have done much to relegate the requirement of *privity of contract* to the ash heap of history.

279. probity

noun

Virtue or integrity tested and confirmed; honesty; the trait of having strong moral principles.

> Once regarded as the model of **probity**, Mayor Bradley, now 71 years old, is under investigation by the City Attorney's Office for possible conflict of interest regarding the Far East deposit and other matters and by the Federal authorities in regard to his connection with Drexel Burnham Lambert Inc., the investment concern that has agreed to plead guilty to charges of financial fraud.
>
> —Robert Reinhold
> "Soul-Searching at *Los Angeles Times*"
> *New York Times*, August 10, 1989

280. prodigious

adjective

Immense, extraordinary in size; wonderful, marvelous.

> America makes **prodigious** mistakes, America has colossal faults, but one thing cannot be denied: America is always on the move. She may be going to Hell, of course, but at least she isn't standing still.
>
> —e. e. cummings
> "Why I Like America"
> *Vanity Fair*, May 1927

281. prodigy

noun

A person, especially a child, with remarkable gifts or qualities; a marvelous example; a wonder.

> Today's pressures on middle-class children to grow up fast begin in early childhood. Chief among them is the pressure for early

> intellectual attainment, deriving from a changed perception of precocity. Several decades ago precocity was looked upon with great suspicion. The child **prodigy**, it was thought, turned out to be a neurotic adult; thus the phrase "early ripe, early rot!"
>
> —David Elkind
> *The Hurried Child* (1988)

282. proffer

verb

To offer to another for acceptance.

noun

The offer itself.

> During my employment of seven years or more in Washington after the war (1865–72) I regularly saved part of my wages: and, though the sum has now become about exhausted by my expenses of the last three years, there are already beginning at present welcome dribbles hitherward from the sales of my new edition, which I just job and sell, myself, (all through this illness, my book-agents for three years in New York successively, badly cheated me,) and shall continue to dispose of the books myself. And that is the way I should prefer to glean my support. In that way I cheerfully accept all the aid my friends find it convenient to **proffer**.
>
> —Walt Whitman
> *Specimen Days & Collect* (1882–83)

283. profligacy, profligate

noun

Profligacy: the trait of spending lavishly or extravagantly; unrestrained indulgence in sensual pleasure.

adjective

Profligate: characterized by wild spending or by engaging in sensual pleasure; as a noun, the person so characterized, a wastrel.

> Upscale people are fixated with food simply because they are now able to eat so much of it without getting fat, and the reason they don't get fat is that they maintain a **profligate** level of calorie expenditure. The very same people whose evenings begin with melted goat's cheese ... get up at dawn to run, break for a mid-morning aerobics class, and watch the evening news while racing on a stationary bicycle.
>
> —Barbara Ehrenreich
> "Food Worship"
> *The Worst Years of Our Lives* (1985)

284. profuse

adjective

Plentiful, copious, abundant; giving or spending freely, often to excess, as in *profuse praise.*

> The little flower which at this season stars our woods and roadsides with its **profuse**

> blooms, might attract even eyes as stern as theirs with its humble beauty.
>
> —Ralph Waldo Emerson
> Speech on the second centennial anniversary of Concord, Massachusetts, September 12, 1835

285. progeny

noun

Descendant, offspring, child; something originating or resulting from something else.

> Preschoolers sound much brighter and more knowledgeable than they really are, which is why so many parents and grandparents are so sure their **progeny** are gifted and super-bright. Because children's questions sound so mature and sophisticated, we are tempted to answer them at a level of abstraction far beyond the child's level of comprehension. That is a temptation we should resist.
>
> —David Elkind
> *Miseducation* (1987)

286. prolific

adjective

Abundantly producing offspring or fruit, as in a *prolific orange tree*; very productive, producing in large quantities.

> Debt is the **prolific** mother of folly and of crime.
>
> —Benjamin Disraeli
> *Henrietta Temple*

287. prolix

adjective

Verbose, wordy, extended to unnecessary and tedious length.

> In a succinct 354 pages (shockingly brief for the normally **prolix** [Susan] Faludi), she argues that in the months and years following the 9/11 attacks, the rhetoric surrounding various notions of national security (some of it appropriate, much of it overly simplistic and reactive) enabled the media to more or less announce that the whole nation was returning to traditional values and gender roles.
>
> —Meghan Daum
> "Did 9/11 Kill Feminism?"
> *Los Angeles Times*, October 6, 2007

288. promulgate

verb

To make known through public declaration; formally proclaim; publish.

Note: In law, we say that Congress ***enacted*** *a statute*. But we say that a federal agency ***promulgated*** *a regulation.*

> One need not be a Scientologist—as I emphatically am not—to advocate for Scientologists' 1st Amendment right to believe their myths, practice their rituals and **promulgate** their message to others. One

> may be a skeptic—as I am—and still marvel at the creative ways in which human societies attain and maintain a collective identity and sense of meaning.
>
> —Jean E. Rosenfeld
> "Scientology Stands a Chance"
> *Los Angeles Times*, February 22, 2008

289. propitious

adjective

Presenting favorable conditions; favorably inclined, auspicious.

> The time is now **propitious**, as he guesses,
> The meal is ended, she is bored and tired,
> Endeavours to engage her in caresses
> Which still are unreproved, if undesired.
> Flushed and decided, he assaults at once;
> Exploring hands encounter no defence.
>
> —T. S. Eliot
> *The Waste Land* (1922)

290. prosaic

adjective

Unimaginative, dull, commonplace, matter-of-fact; vapid; humdrum; tiresome.

> It is better to have a **prosaic** husband and to take a romantic lover.
>
> —Stendhal (Marie Henri Beyle)
> "Various Fragments"
> *De l'Amour* (1822)

291. proscribe

verb

To denounce or condemn something as dangerous or harmful; to prohibit, forbid.

> The public is harmed when lawmakers **proscribe** the use of a product that has been proved safe and useful. Inevitably, manufacturers will turn to—and consumers will be exposed to—alternatives that are likely to be less well tested. Simply put, [Sen. Diane] Feinstein's bill represents bad science, bad law and disregard for the public interest.
>
> —Henry I. Miller
> "Stop Scaring Us: Feinstein's Bill to Ban Some Chemicals in Toys Might Help Rats, But It's Bad for People"
> *Los Angeles Times*, December 18, 2007

292. prostrate

adjective

Lying prone, or with the head to the ground, as in a gesture of humility, adoration, or subservience; physically weak or exhausted; utterly depressed or disconsolate.

verb

To cast oneself on the ground in humility, adoration, or subservience; to reduce to physical weakness; to overcome or reduce to helplessness.

Note: Do not confuse with *prostate*, the male gland that produces the fluid part of semen.

> It is not enough for us to **prostrate** ourselves under the tree which is Creation, and to contemplate its tremendous branches filled with stars. We have a duty to perform, to work upon the human soul, to defend the mystery against the miracle, to worship the incomprehensible while rejecting the absurd; to accept, in the inexplicable, only what is necessary; to dispel the superstitions that surround religion—to rid God of His Maggots.
>
> —Victor Hugo
> *Les Misérables* (1862)

293. prototype

noun

The model or original on which something else is based or formed; a thing or person serving to illustrate typical qualities of a larger class or group; something analogous to a later thing.

> The Ancient Mariner seizes the guest at the wedding feast and will not let go until he has told all his story: the **prototype** of the bore.
>
> —Mason Cooley
> *City Aphorisms* (1989)

294. protract

verb

To prolong, draw out, lengthen the duration of.

Note: The past-participial adjective *protracted* often appears, as in *protracted negotiations*.

> That life **protracted** is **protracted** woe.
>
> —Samuel Johnson
> *The Vanity of Human Wishes: The Tenth Satire of Juvenal Imitated* (1749)

295. proverbial

adjective

Derives from the noun *proverb*, which means a popular saying, usually of ancient and unknown origin, that expresses a commonplace truth. In the Bible, a *proverb* is a profound saying. The word *proverbial* thus means widely referred to, as if the subject of a proverb; commonly referred to, subject to common mention.

> It is far easier for the **proverbial** camel to pass through the needle's eye, hump and all, than for an erstwhile colonial administration to give sound and honest counsel of a political nature to its liberated territory.
>
> —Kwame Nkrumah
> Former President of Ghana
> *Consciencism* (1964)

296. prowess

noun
Exceptional strength, skill, and courage in battle; superior skill or ability.

I am really greatly pleased at your standing so high in your form, and I am sure that this year it is better for you to be playing where you are in football. I suppose next year you will go back to your position of end, as you would hardly be heavy enough for playing back, or to play behind the centre, against teams with big fellows. I repeat that your standing in the class gave me real pleasure. I have sympathized so much with your delight in physical **prowess** and have been so glad at the success you have had, that sometimes I have been afraid I have failed to emphasize sufficiently the fact that of course one must not subordinate study and work to the cultivation of such **prowess**. By the way, I am sorry to say that I am falling behind physically. The last two or three years I have had a tendency to rheumatism, or gout, or something of the kind, which makes me very stiff.

—Theodore Roosevelt
Written from the White House,
October 24, 1903
Theodore Roosevelt's Letters to His Children (Charles Scribner's Sons, 1919)

297. prurient

adjective

Inclined to lascivious or lustful thoughts and desires.

> Nothing is more repulsive than a furtively **prurient** spirituality; it is just as unsavory as gross sensuality.
>
> —Carl Jung
> *Marriage as a Psychological Relationship* (1925)

298. puerile

adjective

Pertaining to childhood; childish, immature, or trivial.

> The idea that leisure is of value in itself is only conditionally true. . . . The average man simply spends his leisure as a dog spends it. His recreations are all **puerile**, and the time supposed to benefit him really only stupefies him.
>
> —H. L. Mencken
> *Minority Report: H.L. Mencken's Notebooks* (1956)

299. punctilious

adjective

Strictly observant of the rules or forms prescribed by law or custom; precise, scrupulous.

> His courtesy was somewhat extravagant. He would write and thank people who wrote to thank him for wedding presents and when he encountered anyone as **punctilious** as himself the correspondence ended only with death.
>
> —Evelyn Waugh

Quoted in "Waugh Stories"
by Joan Acocella
The New Yorker, July 2, 2007

300. punitive

adjective

Pertaining to punishment.

Note: In law, *punitive damages* are awarded in civil suits to punish the wrongdoer and serve as an example to deter others from similar egregious conduct. *Punitive damages* are in excess of the *actual damages* suffered by the injured party.

> In the days ahead I will propose removing the roadblocks that have slowed our economy and reduced productivity. Steps will be taken aimed at restoring the balance between the various levels of government. Progress may be slow—measured in inches and feet, not miles—but we will progress. Is it time to reawaken this industrial giant, to get government back within its means, and to lighten our **punitive** tax burden. And these will be our first priorities, and on these principles, there will be no compromise.
>
> —Former President Ronald Reagan
> First Inaugural Address,
> January 20, 1981

301. purport

noun

The meaning or sense or import, as in *the main purport of the article*; also the purpose or intent, as in *the purport of the trip to Italy.*

verb

To present, especially deliberately, the appearance of being something; to profess or claim, often falsely, as in *the document purporting to be legal.*

> In a secular age, an authentic miracle must **purport** to be a hoax, in order to gain credit in the world.
>
> —Angela Carter
> *Nights at the Circus* (1984)

302. pusillanimous

adjective

Without spirit or bravery; lacking courage; timid; faint-hearted.

> A Prince is despised when he is seen to be fickle, frivolous, effeminate, **pusillanimous**, or irresolute, against which defects he ought therefore most carefully to guard, striving so to bear himself that greatness, courage, wisdom, and strength may appear in all his actions. In his private dealings with his subjects his decisions should be irrevocable, and his reputation such that no one would dream of overreaching or cajoling him.
>
> —Niccolo Machiavelli
> *The Prince* (1513)

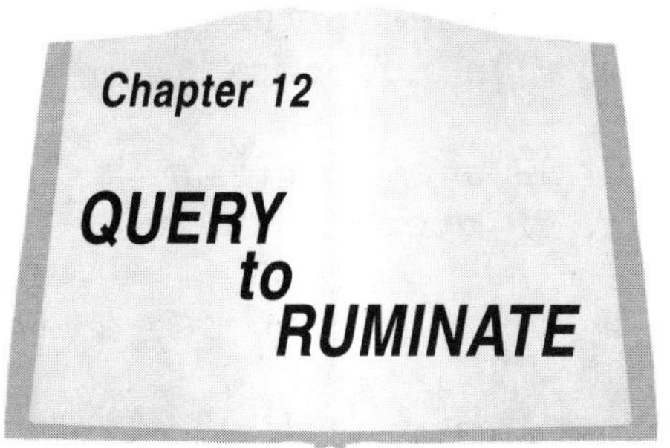

303. query

verb

To inquire, to submit a question.

noun

An inquiry, a question.

> To the **query**, "What is a friend?" his reply was "A single soul dwelling in two bodies."
>
> —Aristotle
> Quoted in *Lives of Eminent Philosophers*, "Aristotle," by Diogenes Laertius

304. queue

verb

To get in line.

noun

A file of persons waiting in order of their arrival, as for admittance.

Note: The word *queue* appears more frequently in Great Britain than in America.

> An Englishman, even if he is alone, forms an orderly **queue** of one.
>
> —George Mikes
> *How to Be an Alien* (1946)

> *Private Lives* was described variously as "tenuous, thin, brittle, gossamer, iridescent and delightfully daring," all of which connoted to the public mind cocktails, evening dress, repartee and irreverent allusions to copulation, thereby causing a gratifying number of respectable people to **queue** up at the box office.
>
> —"'Private Lives' director enjoys play's challenges"
> Play Review of Maury Covington's adaptation of *Private Lives* by Noel Coward (2003)
> *Jacksonville.com,* September 10, 2003

305. quiescent

adjective

Being quiet, at rest, still, motionless, as in *quiescent thoughts.*

> There is a brief time for sex, and a long time when sex is out of place. But when it is out of place as an activity there still should be the large and quiet space in the consciousness where it lives **quiescent**. Old people can have a lovely **quiescent** sort of

> sex, like apples, leaving the young quite free for their sort.
>
> —D. H. Lawrence
> *The Letters of D. H. Lawrence* (1932)

306. quintessence

noun

The most essential part of anything; the pure essence of a substance; the most typical example of something.

> O my lady Dulcinea of Toboso! the sun of all beauty, the end and **quintessence** of discretion, the treasury of sweet countenance and carriage, the storehouse of honesty, and finally, the idea of all that which is profitable, modest, or delightful in the world! and what might thy ladyship be doing at this present? Hast thou perhaps thy mind now upon thy captive knight, that most wittingly exposeth himself to so many dangers for thy sake?
>
> —Miguel de Cervantes
> *Don Quixote* (1605)

307. raillery

noun

Good-humored satire, ridicule, or banter.

> There is a simple but effective test of satire, one that hails back to Aristotle. "Humor is the only test of gravity, and gravity of

> humor," he said, "for a subject which will not bear **raillery** is suspicious, and a jest which will not bear serious examination is false wit."
>
> —Jon Sanders
> "Liberals Don't Get the Joke, But They'll Try to Get the One Who Made It"
> Townhall.com, May 8, 2007

308. rapacious

adjective

Disposed to seize by violence or by unlawful or greedy methods; extremely greedy, predatory, extortionate.

> The American goes to Paris, always has, and comes back and tells his neighbor, always does, how exorbitant and inhospitable it is, how **rapacious** and selfish and unaccommodating and unresponsive it is, how dirty and noisy it is—and the next summer his neighbor goes to Paris.
>
> —Milton Meyer
> "Paris as a State of Mind"
> *New York Times*, June 9, 1985

309. ravenous

adjective

Extremely hungry, voracious, famished.

> The will to domination is a **ravenous** beast. There are never enough warm bodies to

satiate its monstrous hunger. Once alive, this beast grows and grows, feeding on all the life around it, scouring the earth to find new sources of nourishment. This beast lives in each man who battens on female servitude.

—Andrea Dworkin
Our Blood (1976)

310. recant

verb

To formally withdraw or disavow one's belief, position, or statement about something previously believed or maintained.

> I cannot and will not **recant** anything, for to go against conscience is neither right nor safe. Here I stand, I can do no other, so help me God. Amen.
>
> —Martin Luther
> Speech, April 18, 1521

311. recapitulate

verb

To repeat again the principal points of; to summarize.

> "But, for heaven's sake, don't get hot!" said Stepan Arkadyevitch, touching his brother-in-law's knee. "The matter is not ended. If you will allow me to **recapitulate**, it was like this: when you parted, you were as

> magnanimous as could possibly be; you were ready to give her everything—freedom, divorce even. She appreciated that. No, don't think that. She did appreciate it—to such a degree that at the first moment, feeling how she had wronged you, she did not consider and could not consider everything. She gave up everything. But experience, time, have shown that her position is unbearable, impossible."
>
> —Leo Tolstoy
> *Anna Karenin* (1877)

312. recluse

noun

One who lives in seclusion, often for religious meditation.

***Note*:** The adjective form is either *recluse* or *reclusive.*

> Henry David Thoreau and Charles Darwin form both a spectacular comparison and contrast. Both Thoreau and Darwin were voyagers. One confined himself to the ever widening ripples on a pond until they embraced infinity. The other went around the world and remained for the rest of his life a meditative **recluse** in an old Victorian house in the English countryside. . . . Both men were insatiable readers, and composers of works not completely published in their individual lifetimes. Both achieved a passionate satisfaction out of their association with wilderness. Each in his

> individual way has profoundly influenced the lives of generations that followed him.
>
> —Loren Eiseley
> *The Unexpected Universe* (1969)

313. redolent

adjective

Smelling sweet and agreeable; also, suggestive or reminiscent.

Note: The word *redolent* is often followed by the preposition *of.*

> They are very proper forest houses, the stems of the trees collected together and piled up around a man to keep out wind and rain,—made of living green logs, hanging with moss and lichen, and with the curls and fringes of the yellow birch bark, and dripping with resin, fresh and moist, and **redolent** of swampy odors, with that sort of vigor and perennialness even about them that toadstools suggest.
>
> —Henry David Thoreau
> *The Maine Woods* (1864)

314. redoubtable

adjective

Arousing awe or fear, formidable; commanding respect or reverence.

> In "Otto Preminger: The Man Who Would Be King," Brooklyn College film historian Foster Hirsch weaves interviews with industry players and family members into a straightforward chronology of Preminger's wide-ranging career. This comprehensive biography of the **redoubtable** impresario is the first since Preminger's ghostwritten account in 1977. It begins not in Vienna, where Preminger hinted that he was born, but in the "depressed backwater" of Wiznitz, Poland. As the book often demonstrates, circumstance was rarely an obstacle. In 1915, when Otto was 10, his father, an ambitious lawyer, relocated the family to Vienna, where he prosecuted insurgents on behalf of the Austro-Hungarian Empire—a formidable rise, considering that he was a Jew who refused to convert to Catholicism.
>
> —Liz Brown
> Book Review of *Otto Preminger*
> by Foster Hirsch
> *Los Angeles Times*, October 14, 2007

315. regale

verb

To entertain agreeably or lavishly, with food or drink; delight.

Note: The word *regale* also acts as a noun, as in *steaks were grilled for the regale of the guests.*

> Going along the narrow path to a little uncut meadow covered on one side with thick clumps of brilliant heart's-ease among which stood up here and there tall, dark green tufts

> of hellebore, Levin settled his guests in the dense, cool shade of the young aspens on a bench and some stumps purposely put there for visitors to the bee-house who might be afraid of the bees, and he went off himself to the hut to get bread, cucumbers, and fresh honey, to **regale** them with.
>
> —Leo Tolstoy
> *Anna Karenin* (1877)

316. relegate

verb

To send off or consign to an inferior position or remote destination; to assign or commit a task to a person; to banish or exile.

> Children need people in order to become human . . . . It is primarily through observing, playing, and working with others older and younger than himself that a child discovers both what he can do and who he can become—that he develops both his ability and his identity . . . Hence to **relegate** children to a world of their own is to deprive them of their humanity, and ourselves as well.
>
> —Urie Bronfenbrenner
> *Two Worlds of Childhood: U.S. and U.S.S.R.* (1973)

317. remiss

adjective

Negligent, slow, careless in performing a task or duty; also, languid, sluggish.

> Perhaps this hut has never been required to shelter a shipwrecked man, and the benevolent person who promised to inspect it annually, to see that the straw and matches are here, and that the boards will keep off the wind, has grown **remiss** and thinks that storms and shipwrecks are over; and this very night a perishing crew may pry open its door with their numbed fingers and leave half their number dead here by morning. When I thought what must be the condition of the families which alone would ever occupy or had occupied them, what must have been the tragedy of the winter evenings spent by human beings around their hearths, these houses, though they were meant for human dwellings, did not look cheerful to me. They appeared but a stage to the grave.
>
> —Henry David Thoreau
> "Cape Cod"
> *The Writings of Henry David Thoreau* (1906)

318. repertory

noun

A place where things are stored or gathered together, a collection; also, a type of theatrical presentation in which the theater group presents several works.

> Each writer is born with a **repertory** company in his head. Shakespeare has perhaps 20 players, and Tennessee Williams has about 5, and Samuel Beckett one—and

> maybe a clone of that one. I have 10 or so, and that's a lot. As you get older, you become more skillful at casting them.
>
> —Gore Vidal
> *Dallas Times Herald*, June 18, 1978

319. replete

adjective

Full to the uttermost, abundantly provided or supplied, filled with; complete, as in *a legal brief replete in its citations to authority.*

> The highway is **replete** with culinary land mines disguised as quaint local restaurants that carry such reassuring names as Millie's, Pop's and Capt'n Dick's.
>
> —Bryan Miller
> "Never Eat at Mom's"
> *New York Times*, July 16, 1983

320. repute

noun

Estimation in the view of others; reputation, as in *a house of ill repute.*

verb

To believe a person or thing to be as specified; to regard.

Note: The verb form *repute* usually appears in the passive voice, as in *he was reputed to be quite wealthy.*

> Women are **reputed** never to be disgusted. The sad fact is that they often are, but not with men; following the lead of men, they are most often disgusted with themselves.
>
> —Germaine Greer
> *The Female Eunuch* (1970)

321. requisite

noun

A required thing, something necessary or indispensable.

adjective

Necessary or required for a particular purpose, as in *the requisite skills.*

> No wealth can buy the **requisite** leisure, freedom, and independence which are the capital in this profession. It comes only by the grace of God. It requires a direct dispensation from Heaven to become a walker. You must be born into the family of the Walkers.
>
> —Henry David Thoreau, "Walking"
> *The Writings of Henry David Thoreau* (1906)

322. respite

noun
Interval of rest; a delay or cessation of anything trying or distressing.

> Whatever choice Elizabeth Bouvia may ultimately make, I can only hope that her

> courage, persistence and example will cause our society to deal realistically with the plight of those unfortunate individuals to whom death beckons as a welcome **respite** from suffering.
>
> —Judge Lynn Compton,
> California Court of Appeals
> From a unanimous court opinion
> on the right to refuse medical treatment,
> April 16, 1986

323. resplendent

adjective

Very bright, shining brightly, gleaming, splendid, as in *the dancers resplendent in their native costumes*.

> In the luxuriance of a bowl of grapes set out in ritual display, in a bottle of wine, the soil and sunshine of California reached millions for whom that distant place would henceforth be envisioned as a sun-graced land **resplendent** with the goodness of the fruitful earth.
>
> —Kevin Starr
> *Inventing the Dream: California Through the Progressive Era* (1985)

324. reticence, reticent

noun

Reticence: the quality of habitually keeping silent or being reserved in utterance.

adjective

Reticent: disposed to be silent or reserved

> Ted had come down from the University for the week-end. Though he no longer spoke of mechanical engineering and though he was **reticent** about his opinion of his instructors, he seemed no more reconciled to college, and his chief interest was his wireless telephone set.
>
> —Sinclair Lewis
> *Babbitt* (1922)

325. retroactive

adjective

Operative on, affecting, or having reference to past events, transactions, responsibilities; pertaining to a pay raise effective in the past.

> In June, the Judiciary Committee subpoenaed the documents underlying the warrantless surveillance program, and Chairman Patrick J. Leahy (D-Vt.) and ranking Republican Arlen Specter (Pa.) said they wanted to see those documents before endorsing any immunity clause. "I'm not going to buy a pig in a poke and commit to **retroactive** immunity when I don't know what went on" in the past, Specter said Tuesday on CNN's "Situation Room." "I agree with Arlen," Leahy said on the program.
>
> —Jonathan Weisman
> and Ellen Nakashima

"Senate and Bush Agree
on Terms of Spying Bill"
Washington Post, October 18, 2007

326. retrospective

noun

An exhibition of art or performance of works produced by an artist or composer over time.

adjective

Directed to past events or situations; looking backward, looking back on.

> The university must be **retrospective**. The gale that gives direction to the vanes on all its towers blows out of antiquity.
>
> —Ralph Waldo Emerson
> "Universities"
> *English Traits* (1856)

327. revile

verb

To address or speak of with abuse; vilify, berate, disparage.

> You shall not **revile** God, or curse a leader of your people.
>
> —Exodus 22:28
> Old Testament

328. rife

adjective

Of frequent or common occurrence; in widespread existence, prevalent, use, or activity; abundant, numerous, plentiful.

> I love to see that Nature is so **rife** with life that myriads can be afforded to be sacrificed and suffered to prey on one another; that tender organizations can be so serenely squashed out of existence like pulp.
>
> —Henry David Thoreau
> "Walden"
> *The Writings of Henry David Thoreau* (1906)

329. ruminate

verb

To chew over again, as food previously swallowed and regurgitated; to meditate about, ponder.

> Let's start with their explication of depression, which has metastasized in the West over the past two generations. Victims can see that Griffin and Tyrrell know why they wake up exhausted and unmotivated. This alone gives hope. Somebody finally understands what has long baffled the patient—that peace eludes him even when asleep, and that psychotherapy based on **ruminating** about past miseries makes depression worse.
>
> —Lou Marano
> "Civilization: Psychology Breakthrough"
> *Washington Times*, October 9, 2003

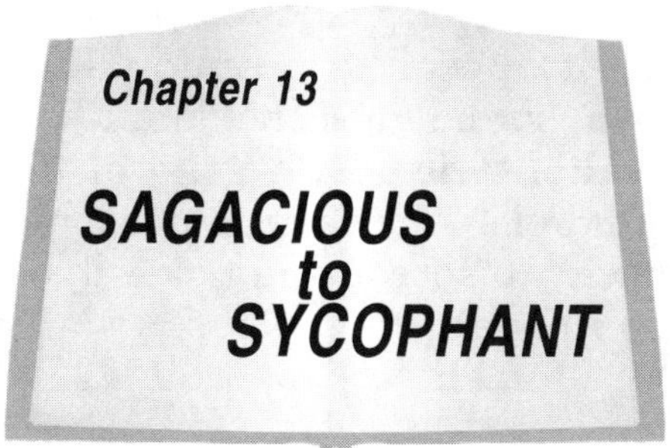

330. sagacious

adjective

Able to discern and distinguish with wise perception; having a keen practical sense.

> What arouses the indignation of the honest satirist is not, unless the man is a prig, the fact that people in positions of power or influence behave idiotically, or even that they behave wickedly. It is that they conspire successfully to impose upon the public a picture of themselves as so very **sagacious**, honest and well-intentioned.
>
> —Claud Cockburn
> "The Worst Possible Taste"
> *Cockburn Sums Up* (1981)

331. salient

adjective

Conspicuous or prominent; projecting or pointing outward; springing, jumping.

> Has the art of politics no apparent utility? Does it appear to be unqualifiedly ratty, raffish, sordid, obscene, and low down, and its **salient** virtuosi a gang of unmitigated scoundrels? Then let us not forget its high capacity to soothe and tickle the midriff, its incomparable services as a maker of entertainment.
>
> —H. L. Mencken
> *A Carnival of Buncombe* (1956)

332. salutary

adjective

Promoting or favorable to health, healthful; promoting some beneficial purpose, wholesome; designed to effect improvement.

> Columbus stood in his age as the pioneer of progress and enlightenment. The system of universal education is in our age the most prominent and **salutary** feature of the spirit of enlightenment, and it is peculiarly appropriate that the schools be made by the people the center of the day's demonstration. Let the national flag float over every schoolhouse in the country and the exercises be such as shall impress upon our youth the patriotic duties of American citizenship.
>
> —Former President Benjamin Harrison
> Presidential Proclamation, July 21, 1892
> *A Compilation of the Messages and Papers of the Presidents, 1789-1897* (GPO 1898)

333. sanctimonious

adjective

Making an ostentatious display or hypocritical pretense of holiness, piety, or righteousness.

> Recently, I boarded a flight from Boston to New York. As I sat down, the attendant announced that the flight was scheduled to take less than two hours (it actually took four hours) and consequently "in accord with Federal Aviation Association regulations this is a nonsmoking flight." A large number of the passengers cheered and applauded.
>
> There was something so **sanctimonious** about this outburst that I spent the remainder of the flight trying to understand why. I concluded that I had witnessed a self-righteous exhibition of moral superiority. This is not something most people, in these days of subjective moral values, have much opportunity to do. However, smoking has now become a sin, so opposing it has taken on a sanctioned and religious quality.
>
> —David Scott Davis
> "Selfish, **Sanctimonious** Anti-Smokers"
> *New York Times*, January 27, 1989

334. sanguine

adjective

Optimistic (and cheerfully so), hopeful, confident; reddish, ruddy.

Note: Do not confuse *sanguine* with *sanguinary*. *Sanguinary* means "bloodthirsty" or "accompanied by bloodshed."

How did two seemingly different meanings arise? According to medieval physiology, the body had four humors or bodily fluids (blood, bile, phlegm, and black bile). As these fluids varied in proportion so did a person's temperament. If blood predominated, a person had a ruddy face, which showed courage, hope, and a predisposition to fall in love. This temperament was called *sanguine*.

335. sardonic

adjective

Scornfully or bitterly sarcastic, mocking, cynical, sneering.

> Freud, Jung thought, had been a great discoverer of facts about the mind, but far too inclined to leave the solid ground of "critical reason and common sense." Freud for his part criticized Jung for being gullible about occult phenomena and infatuated with Oriental religions; he viewed with **sardonic** and unmitigated skepticism Jung's defense of religious feelings as an integral element in mental health. For Freud, religion was a psychological need projected onto culture, the child's feeling of helplessness surviving in adults, to be analyzed rather than admired.
>
> —Peter Gay
> "Psychoanalytical Politics"
> *Freud: A Life for Our Time* (1988)

336. satiate

verb

To satisfy fully the appetite or desire of; to satisfy to excess.

> I am no longer sure of anything. If I **satiate** my desires, I sin but I deliver myself from them; if I refuse to satisfy them, they infect the whole soul.
>
> —Jean-Paul Sartre
> *The Devil and the Good Lord* (1951)

337. scurrilous

adjective

Grossly abusive; expressed in coarse, vulgar language.

> Every two years the American politics industry fills the airwaves with the most virulent, **scurrilous**, wall-to-wall character assassination of nearly every political practitioner in the country—and then declares itself puzzled that America has lost trust in its politicians.
>
> —Charles Krauthammer
> *Chicago Tribune*, October 28, 1994

338. sibilant

adjective

Characterized by a hissing sound; in phonetics,

noting sounds like those spelled with *s*, *sh*, *z*, *zh*, as in *a sibilant consonant*.

noun

Sibilant speech sound.

> When anybody entered the room, she uttered a *shshshsh* so ***sibilant*** and ominous, that it frightened the poor old lady in her bed, from which she could not look without seeing Mrs. Bute's beady eyes eagerly fixed on her, as the latter sat steadfast in the arm-chair by the bedside.
>
> —William M. Thackeray
> *Vanity Fair* (1917)

339. simile

noun

A figure of speech in which two dissimilar things are explicitly compared, often introduced with *like* or *as*, as in *she runs like the wind*.

> **Simile** and Metaphor differ only in degree of stylistic refinement. The **Simile**, in which a comparison is made directly between two objects, belongs to an earlier stage of literary expression; it is the deliberate elaboration of a correspondence, often pursued for its own sake. But a Metaphor is the swift illumination of an equivalence. Two images, or an idea and an image, stand equal and opposite; clash together and respond

significantly, surprising the reader with a sudden light.

—Sir Herbert Read
English Prose Style (1928)

340. similitude

noun

Similarity, likeness, resemblance; a person or thing that is the match or like another.

> When he had a mind to penetrate into the inclinations of those he had to deal with, he composed his face, his gesture, and his whole body, as nearly as he could into the exact **similitude** of the person he intended to examine; and then carefully observed what turn of mind he seemed to acquire by this change.
>
> —Edmund Burke
> *On the Sublime and Beautiful* (1756)

341. solecism

noun

A nonstandard or ungrammatical usage, as in *There's lots of cars on the road*; a breach of good manners.

***Note*:** The single most prevalent **solecism** in America consists of using *there is* followed by a plural noun (see example above). For more, visit Grammar.com and use GrammaRight—Clickable Help for Writers.

342. somnolent

adjective
Tending to produce sleep; drowsy, sleepy.

> Gringoire, stunned by his fall, lay prone upon the pavement in front of the image of Our Lady at the corner of the street. By slow degrees his senses returned, but for some moments he lay in a kind of **half-somnolent** state—not without its charms—in which the airy figures of the gipsy and her goat mingled strangely with the weight of Quasimodo's fist. This condition, however, was of short duration.
>
> —Victor Hugo
> *Notre Dame de Paris* (1831)

343. sophistry

noun

A false, tricky but plausible argument understood to be such by the speaker himself and intentionally used to deceive.

> . . . that phrase of mischievous **sophistry**, "all men are born free and equal." This false and futile axiom, which has done, is doing, and will do so much harm to this fine country.
>
> —Frances Trollope
> *Domestic Manners of the Americans* (1832)

344. spurious

adjective

Not genuine, authentic, or true; not from the pretended or proper source; counterfeit.

> Jargon is the verbal sleight of hand that makes the old hat seem newly fashionable; it gives an air of novelty and specious profundity to ideas that, if stated directly, would seem superficial, stale, frivolous, or false. The line between serious and **spurious** scholarship is an easy one to blur, with jargon on your side.
>
> —David Lehman
> *Signs of the Times* (1991)

345. stolid

adjective

Revealing or having little emotion or sensibility; impassive; unemotional.

> The Indian sat on the front seat, saying nothing to anybody, with a **stolid** expression of face, as if barely awake to what was going on. Again I was struck by the peculiar vagueness of his replies when addressed in the stage, or at the taverns. He really never said anything on such occasions. He was merely stirred up, like a wild beast, and passively muttered some insignificant response. His answer, in such cases, was never the consequence of a positive mental energy, but vague as a puff of smoke, suggesting no responsibility, and if you considered it, you would find that you had got nothing out of him. This was instead of

> the conventional palaver and smartness of the white man, and equally profitable.
>
> —Henry David Thoreau
> "The Allegash and East Branch"
> *The Maine Woods* (1864)
> *The Writings of Henry David Thoreau* (1906)

348. stultify

verb

To give an appearance of foolishness to; to render wholly futile or ineffectual, usually in a degrading or frustrating way.

> A calm virility and a dreamy humor, marked contrasts to her level-headedness—into these moods she slipped sometimes as a refuge. She could do the most prosy things (though she was wise enough never to **stultify** herself with such "household arts" as knitting and embroidery), yet immediately afterward pick up a book and let her imagination rove as a formless cloud with the wind. Deepest of all in her personality was the golden radiance that she diffused around her. As an open fire in a dark room throws romance and pathos into the quiet faces at its edge, so she cast her lights and shadows around the rooms that held her, until she made of her prosy old uncle a man of quaint and meditative charm, metamorphosed the stray telegraph boy into a Puck-like creature of delightful originality.
>
> —F. Scott Fitzgerald
> *This Side of Paradise* (1920)

347. suasion

noun

The act of urging, advising, or persuading; an instance of persuasion.

> All gentle cant and philosophizing to the contrary notwithstanding, no people in this world ever did achieve their freedom by goody-goody talk and moral **suasion**: it being immutable law that all revolutions that will succeed, must begin in blood.
>
> —Mark Twain
> *A Connecticut Yankee in King Arthur's Court* (1889)

348. subjugate

verb

To bring under total control or subjection; to conquer, master, or enslave.

> To ask strength not to express itself as strength, not to be a will to dominate, a will to **subjugate**, a will to become master, a thirst for enemies and obstacles and triumphant celebrations, is just as absurd as to ask weakness to express itself as strength.
>
> —Friedrich Nietzsche
> "First Essay"
> *On the Genealogy of Morals* (1887)

349. substantive

adjective

Belonging to the real nature of a thing, essential; possessing substance, having practical importance. In law, *substantive* pertains to provisions of law dealing with rights and duties, as distinguished from *procedural* provisions, which dictate procedures in court.

Note: The accent falls on the first syllable of this word, as in *SUBstuhntive*, not *subSTANtive.*

> You can't remember sex. You can remember the fact of it, and recall the setting, and even the details, but the sex of the sex cannot be remembered, the **substantive** truth of it, it is by nature self-erasing, you can remember its anatomy and be left with a judgment as to the degree of your liking of it, but whatever it is as a splurge of being, as a loss, as a charge of the conviction of love stopping your heart like your execution, there is no memory of it in the brain, only the deduction that it happened and that time passed, leaving you with a silhouette that you want to fill in again.
>
> —E. L. Doctorow
> *Billy Bathgate* (1989)

350. subterfuge

noun

A device or conduct used to evade a rule, escape a consequence, or hide a course of conduct;

something used to hide the true nature of conduct or event.

> Men felt a chill in their hearts; a damp in their minds. In a desperate effort to snuggle their feelings into some sort of warmth, one **subterfuge** was tried after another ... sentences swelled, adjectives multiplied, lyrics became epics.
>
> —Virginia Woolf
> *Orlando* (1928)

351. superсilious

adjective

Exhibiting haughty, arrogant contempt or superiority for those considered unworthy.

> In a quick turn of her head, in a frank look, a boyish pout, in that proud glance from lowered lids, so pitying and yet so distant that in others it would be **supercilious**, in all those expressions of conscious beauty, which when imitated become clumsy, or arrogant, or ridiculous, there is a manifestation of what Hollywood cannot destroy. In the presence of this mystery all that is second-rate can be forgotten.
>
> —Sir Cecil Beaton, Society Photographer
> Describing Gretta Garbo

352. superfluous

adjective

Being more than is needed or sufficient; excess.

Superfluous wealth can buy superfluities only. Money is not required to buy one necessary of the soul.

—Henry David Thoreau
"Conclusion"
Walden (1854)

353. supplant

verb

To force out another, through strategy or schemes; to take the place of.

> Socialists propose to **supplant** the competitive planning of capitalism with a highly centralized planned economy. Our aim is frankly international and not narrowly patriotic (Daughters of the American Revolution please notice), but I cannot here discuss socialism's international policies.
>
> If we gained control of the American Government, we would probably begin with a complete revision of the national governmental system. We would do one of two things. We would write an amendment to the Constitution giving the Federal Government the right to regulate all private business and to enter into any business which it deemed proper, or we would abolish the Constitution altogether and give the National Congress the power to interpret the people's will subject only to certain general principles of free speech and free assemblage.
>
> —Paul Blanshard
> "Socialist and Capitalist Planning"
> *The Annals of the American Academy of Political and Social Science*, July 1932

354. supposition

noun

Conjecture, assumption; something that is supposed; an opinion based on incomplete evidence.

> Another and far more important reason than the delivery of a pair of embroidered gloves impelled Hester, at this time, to seek an interview with a personage of so much power and activity in the affairs of the settlement. It had reached her ears, that there was a design on the part of some of the leading inhabitants, cherishing the more rigid order of principles in religion and government, to deprive her of her child. On the **supposition** that Pearl, as already hinted, was of demon origin, these good people not unreasonably argued that a Christian interest in the mother's soul required them to remove such a stumbling-block from her path. If the child, on the other hand, were really capable of moral and religious growth, and possessed the elements of ultimate salvation, then, surely, it would enjoy all the fairer prospect of these advantages by being transferred to wiser and better guardianship than Hester Prynne's.
>
> —Nathaniel Hawthorne
> *The Scarlet Letter* (1850)

355. surfeit

noun

Excess, an excessive amount, as in *a surfeit of*

political speeches; overindulgence in eating and drinking; general disgust caused by excess.

verb

To supply with anything to excess; to feed to fullness or satiety.

> At banquets **surfeit** not, but fill; partake, and retire; and eat not again till you crave.
>
> —Herman Melville
>
> *Mardi* (1849)

356. surrogate

noun

A person appointed to act for another, a deputy; a substitute; a *surrogate mother*. In law, in some states, a *surrogate* is a judicial officer charged with probating wills and administering estates.

As an adjective, regarded as, or acting as, a surrogate.

> Reading is merely a **surrogate** for thinking for yourself; it means letting someone else direct your thoughts. Many books, moreover, serve merely to show how many ways there are of being wrong, and how far astray you yourself would go if you followed their guidance. You should read only when your own thoughts dry up, which will of course happen frequently enough even to the best heads; but to banish your own thoughts so as to take up a book is a sin against the holy ghost; it is like deserting untrammeled

nature to look at a herbarium or engravings of landscapes.

—Arthur Schopenhauer
"On Thinking for Yourself"
Essays and Aphorisms, (1970)

357. sycophant

noun

A servile flatterer, especially of those in authority or influence; a fawning parasite.

> Your future connection with Britain, whom you can neither love nor honour, will be forced and unnatural, and being formed only on the plan of present convenience, will in a little time fall into a relapse more wretched than the first. But if you say, you can still pass the violations over, then I ask, Hath your house been burnt? Hath your property been destroyed before your face? Are your wife and children destitute of a bed to lie on, or bread to live on? Have you lost a parent or a child by their hands, and yourself the ruined and wretched survivor? If you have not, then are you not a judge of those who have. But if you have, and still can shake hands with the murderers, then you are unworthy of the name of husband, father, friend, or lover, and whatever may be your rank or title in life, you have the heart of a coward, and the spirit of a **sycophant**.
>
> —Thomas Paine
> *Common Sense* (1776)

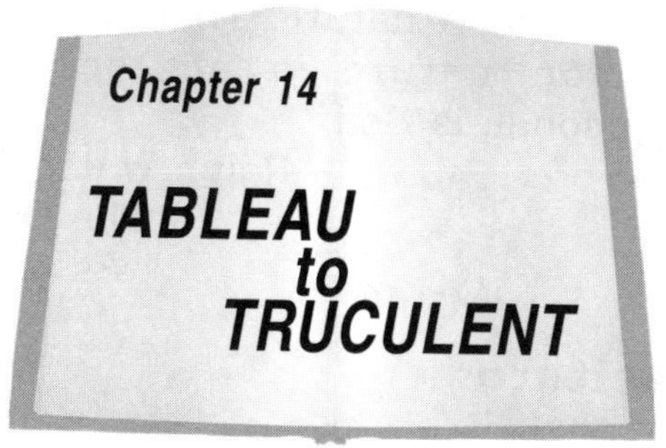

358. tableau

noun

A picture, of a scene; a vivid description; an arrangement of inanimate figures representing a scene from real life, all costumed and posed. In a play, a time in a scene when all actors freeze and then resume the action.

> The simple **tableau** is so rich with meaning that whether represented on the mantelpiece or in the mind, it seems suspended, complete unto itself, somewhere in eternity.
>
> —Lucinda Franks
> "Pilgrimage"
> *New York Times*, December 23, 1984

359. tacit

adjective

Understood, without being expressed; implied, as in *a tacit agreement*; silent, as in *a tacit partner.*

> In all conversation between two persons, **tacit** reference is made, as to a third party,

> to a common nature. That third party or common nature is not social; it is impersonal; is God.
>
> —Ralph Waldo Emerson
> "The Over-Soul"
> *Essays* (1841)

360. taciturn

adjective

Disinclined to conversation; reserved in speech; not talkative.

> Nature is garrulous to the point of confusion, let the artist be truly **taciturn**.
>
> —Paul Klee
> *The Diaries of Paul Klee* (1965)

361. tangible

adjective

Perceptible by touch; material or substantial; real, actual, not imaginary, not vague.

Note: A *tangible asset* is something you can see and touch and, you hope, sell. Examples include gold bars, silver coins, houses, and land.

362. tantamount

adjective

Equivalent to (but not the same as), amounts to, might as well be the same as.

> Most women of [the World War II] generation

> have but one image of good motherhood—the one their mothers embodied. . . . Anything done "for the sake of the children" justified, even ennobled the mother's role. Motherhood was **tantamount** to martyrdom during that unique era when children were gods. Those who appeared to put their own needs first were castigated and shunned—the ultimate damnation for a gender trained to be wholly dependent on the acceptance and praise of others.
>
> —Melinda M. Marshall
> *Good Enough Mothers* (1993)

363. temerity

noun

Recklessness, boldness, rashness; fearless daring.

> The old man trusts wholly to slow contrivance and gradual progression; the youth expects to force his way by genius, vigour, and precipitance. The old man pays regard to riches, and the youth reverences virtue. The old man defies prudence; the youth commits himself to magnanimity and chance. The young man, who intends no ill, believes that none is intended, and therefore acts with openness and candour: but his father, having suffered the injuries of fraud, is impelled to suspect, and too often allured to practice it. Age looks with anger on the **temerity** of youth, and youth with contempt on the scrupulosity of age.
>
> —Samuel Johnson
> *Rasselas* (1759)

364. temporize

verb

To gain time or delay acting by being indecisive or evasive; to comply with the time or the occasion, to yield ostensibly to current opinion; to produce a compromise; to come to terms.

> The third European peace is within reach and the fourth can be set on course with timely action at the Bucharest summit. If, instead, we **temporize**, we will cast doubt on what America stands for and on the strength and unity of the Europe that is being built before our eyes.
>
> —Bruce P. Jackson
> "At NATO, No Time for Cold Feet"
> *Washington Post*, February 4, 2008

365. tenacious

adjective

Unyielding, holding fast, keeping a firm grip, stubborn, obstinate.

> Isabel was perfectly aware that she had not taken the measure of Pansy's **tenacity**, which might prove to be inconveniently great; but she inclined to think the young girl would not be **tenacious**, for she had the faculty of assent developed in a very much higher degree than that of resistance. She would cling, yes, she would cling; but it really mattered to her very little what she clung to.
>
> —Henry James
> *The Portrait of a Lady* (1908)

366. tenet

noun

An opinion, principle, dogma, or doctrine a person or group believes or maintains as true.

> A central **tenet** of modern feminist thought has been the assertion that "all women are oppressed." This assertion implies that women share a common lot, that factors like class, race, religion, sexual preference, etc. do not create a diversity of experience that determines the extent to which sexism will be an oppressive force in the lives of individual women.
>
> —Bell Hooks
> *Feminist Theory* (1984)

367. therefore, therefor

adverb

Therefore: serves as a conjunctive adverb or as a regular adverb. When it joins two clauses, it must be preceded by a semicolon and followed by a comma: *The court upheld the lower court; therefore, the appellant lost once again.* When it serves as a regular adverb, it needs no commas if you want to stress its modification of the verb: *The court therefore ignored these arguments.*

Therefor: a regular adverb that never joins clauses. It means "for it" or "for that thing or action." It might appear like this: *She earned millions for her company but was never compensated therefor.*

368. torpor

noun

Apathy, sluggish inactivity, a state of suspended physical activity, lethargic indifference.

> Nothing is so well calculated to produce a death-like **torpor** in the country as an extended system of taxation and a great national debt.
>
> —William Cobbett
> Letter, February 10, 1804

369. tortious, tortuous, torturous

noun

Tortious: a legal word that refers to an act that gives ground for a lawsuit based on tort law.

adjective

***Note*:** The words *torturous* and *tortuous* come from the same Latin root "torquere," which means "to twist." But their meanings today are distinct.

Torturous: related to the word *torture*, which means "to inflict pain." In rare cases, it also means "twisted."

Tortuous: "winding," "twisting," or sometimes "complex."

> ***Torturous*** refers specifically to what involves or causes pain or suffering:

> *prisoners working in the* ***torturous*** *heat;* ***torturous*** *memories of past injustice.* Some speakers and writers use torturous for ***tortuous***, especially in the senses "twisting, winding" and "convoluted": *a* ***torturous*** *road;* ***torturous*** *descriptions.* Others, however, keep the two adjectives (and their corresponding adverbs) separate in all senses: *a* ***tortuous*** (twisting) road; **tortuous** (convoluted) descriptions; ***torturous*** (painful) treatments.
>
> —Dictionary.reference.com/ browse/torturous

***Example*:** Without power steering, the **tortuous** road was **torturous** to drive in the old truck, and the injured bystanders claimed that maintaining the truck in a dilapidated condition constituted a **tortious** act.

370. tractable

adjective

Easily led or controlled, as in *a tractable child* or *tractable voters.*

> The parole board scene, like many other sequences here, attests to the filmmakers' skill at unobtrusively entering the prisoners' world and at avoiding trite, melodramatic ideas about incarceration. No cafeteria fights or tin cups banging bars here; the inmates have become a **tractable** group thanks to the virtual hopelessness of their situation.

> Some, like the model prisoner Ashanti Witherspoon, who was sentenced to 75 years for armed robbery and now counsels new inmates about what they can expect, have become the helpful citizens they never were before. All speak of their past crimes as if they were part of a separate life.
>
> — Janet Maslin
> Film Review of *The Farm* (1998)
> *New York Times*, June 10, 1998

371. transitive verb

Note: The *transitive verb* is a good thing to know. Since many experienced writers usually know its ins and outs, I've included a brief discussion here. For more, I invite you to visit my website at Grammar.com and download GrammaRight—Clickable Help for Writers.

Here's an excerpt from GrammaRight:

Verbs with Objects
As Amber and Igor [our prehistoric grammarians] became grammatically aware, Amber noticed that action verbs came in two models. One described someone (the subject) doing something (the verb) to someone or something (the direct object). Thus:

- The spear (subject) snagged (verb) the fish (direct object).
- John (subject) hit (verb) the ball (direct object).

These short, simple, three-part sentences seem limitless:

Three-Part Sentences with Transitive Action Verbs

Subject	Verb	Direct Object
1. Mary	2. wrote	3. the novel.
1. The court	2. decides	3. the *case.*
1. The doctor	2. removed	3. the tumor.
1. The criminal	2. broke	3. the law.
1. The politician	2. will dodge	3. the question.

So way back at the dawn of grammatical time, Amber and Igor noticed that, among all the action verbs they had created, most had the capability of sticking directly to a noun. These action verbs could seemingly *pick up* a noun all by themselves. *Write* could pick up *book. Hit* could pick up *ball. Snag* could pick up *fish.*

To name these kinds of action verbs, Amber and Igor first grunted:

- noun-picker-upper!

For they knew that this most prevalent of the action verbs had the unique ability to pick up a noun and complete the action of the verb: *John* (the do-er) *hit* (the action) *the ball* (the do-ee). But because the term noun-*picker-upper* would never survive in the faculty lounge, our ancient grammarians went back to the drawing board and then grunted:

- transitive verb!

Much better.

To be admitted to The Writers' Club, you must know what a transitive verb is. You must know that it's an action verb. You must know that it's an action verb that can pick up a noun all by itself. You must know that you can stick a noun directly on the transitive verb. And you must know the name of that noun: direct object. . . . .

Why is it important to know what a transitive verb is? Two reasons.

First, when we study the active and passive voices, you'll learn that only transitive verbs can appear in the passive voice. Second, if you go around grunting noun-picker-upper all the time, you'll never make it in the faculty lounge.

Your understanding of the transitive verb will grow when you fully comprehend its opposite, the intransitive verb.

. . . . For more, visit Grammar.com and download GrammaRight to your computer.

372. travail

noun

Hard or agonizing labor, painfully difficult work; anguish or suffering resulting from physical or mental hardship; also, the pain of childbirth.

> Far travel, very far travel, or **travail**, comes near to the worth of staying at home.
>
> —Henry David Thoreau
> *Walden* (1864)

373. travesty

noun

A burlesque of a serious work characterized by grotesque incompatibility of style of the original; a grotesque imitation, as in *a travesty of justice.*

Note: Though *travesty* is often used to mean "a gross injustice," perhaps from the popular saying "a travesty of justice," it actually means a grotesque imitation. Consider the example from the *New York Times*. The opening sentence uses *travesty* to mean not "grotesque imitation" but "injustice" or "big mistake." Compare the first example with the second, which uses the term properly.

> **1.** What was the biggest **travesty** of the 80th annual Oscars? Did your movie get nominated and then doinked? Or perhaps it never made it to the show? Or maybe a character portrayal left you stapled to your seat, but never gained traction in the awards narrative?
>
> —David Carr
> "Kvetching Toward Bethlehem"
> The Carpetbagger Blog
> *New York Times*, February 26, 2008

> **2.** Interior design is a **travesty** of the architectural process and a frightening condemnation of the credulity, helplessness and gullibility of the most formidable consumers—the rich.
>
> —Stephen Bayley
> "Interiors: Vacuums of Taste"
> *Taste* (1991)

374. trepidation

noun

Nervous uncertainty of feeling; tremulous alarm, fear; quivering movement.

> Immediately after dinner Kitty came in. She knew Anna Arkadyevna, but only very slightly, and she came now to her sister's with some **trepidation**, at the prospect of meeting this fashionable Petersburg lady, whom every one spoke so highly of. But she made a favourable impression on Anna Arkadyevna—she saw that at once. Anna was unmistakably admiring her loveliness and her youth: before Kitty knew where she was she found herself not merely under Anna's sway, but in love with her, as young girls do fall in love with older and married women.
>
> —Leo Tolstoy
> *Anna Karenin* (1877)

375. truculent

adjective

Fiercely brutal, cruel, vitriolic, scathing, belligerent.

> The past is present everywhere, but Japan is an unusually history-haunted nation. Elsewhere the Cold War is spoken of in the past tense. Japan, however, lives in a dangerous neighborhood with two communist regimes—**truculent** China and weird North Korea. For Japan, the fall of the

Berlin Wall did not close an epoch. Even World War II still shapes political discourse because of a Shinto shrine in the center of this city [Tokyo].

Young soldiers leaving Japan during that war often would say, "If I don't come home, I'll see you at Yasukuni." The souls of 2.5 million casualties of Japan's wars are believed to be present at that shrine. In 1978, 14 other souls were enshrined there—those of 14 major war criminals.

—George F. Will
"The Uneasy Sleep of Japan's Dead"
Washington Post, August 20, 2006

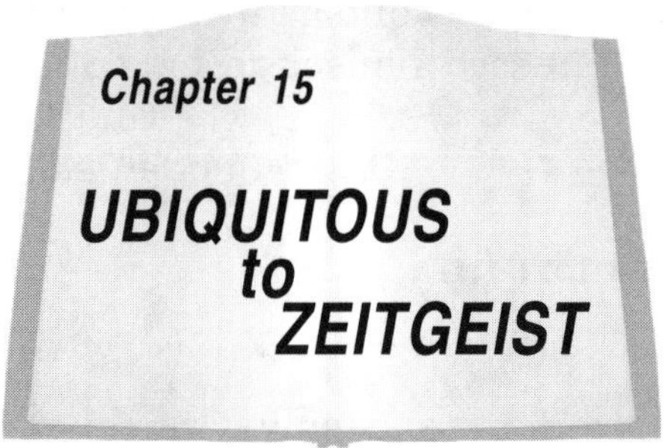

376. ubiquitous

adjective

Being present everywhere, omnipresent.

> Hardly a section of the country, urban or rural, has escaped the **ubiquitous** presence of ragged, ill and hallucinating human beings, wandering through our city streets, huddled in alleyways or sleeping over vents.
>
> —American Psychiatric Association
> *New York Times*, September 13, 1984

377. umbrage

noun

A sense of injury, annoyance, offense, injury; vague feel of doubt or suspicion; leaves affording shade, shade, or shadows cast by trees.

> Mr. Jack Maldon shook hands with me; but not very warmly, I believed; and with an air of languid patronage, at which I secretly took great **umbrage**. But his languor altogether

> was quite a wonderful sight; except when he addressed himself to his cousin Annie.
>
> —Charles Dickens
> *David Copperfield* (1848–50)

378. unctuous

adjective

Characterized by excessive moralistic fervor, especially in an affected manner; excessively smooth or smug; characteristic of an unguent or oil, oily, greasy; abundant in organic material, as in *unctuous soil.*

> Congress—these, for the most part, illiterate hacks whose fancy vests are spotted with gravy and whose speeches, hypocritical, **unctuous** and slovenly, are spotted also with the gravy of political patronage.
>
> —Mary McCarthy
> *On the Contrary* (1961)

379. unique

adjective

Being the only one of its kind.

Note: Be careful and refrain from using adverbs to modify *unique*, such as *very unique, the most unique, extremely unique. Unique* means *unique.* One exception: *almost unique.* But consider this contrary view from Dictionary. com:

> Many authors of usage guides, editors, teachers, and others feel strongly that such "absolute" words as *complete, equal, perfect,* and especially *unique* cannot be compared

> because of their "meaning": a word that denotes an absolute condition cannot be described as denoting more or less than that absolute condition. However, all such words have undergone semantic development and are used in a number of senses, some of which can be compared by words like *more, very, most, absolutely, somewhat,* and *totally* and some of which cannot.
>
> The earliest meanings of *unique* when it entered English around the beginning of the 17th century were "single, sole" and "having no equal." By the mid-19th century *unique* had developed a wider meaning, "not typical, unusual," and it is in this wider sense that it is compared: *The foliage on the late-blooming plants is more unique than that on the earlier varieties.* The comparison of so-called absolutes in senses that are not absolute is standard in all varieties of speech and writing.

I like to follow the advice of Bryan Garner in *The Oxford Dictionary of American Usage and Style* 338 (2000):

> Strictly speaking, **unique** means "being one of a kind," not "unusual." Hence, the phrases *very unique, quite unique, how unique,* and the like are slovenly. The *OED* [*Oxford English Dictionary*] notes that this tendency to hyperbole—to use *unique* when all that it means is "uncommon, unusual, remarkable"—began in the 19th century. However old it is, the tendency is worth resisting.
>
> But who can demand responsible use of the language from an ad writer who is loose

enough to say, in a national advertisement, that a certain luxury sedan is "so unique, it's capable of thought"? And what are we to make of the following examples?

- "This year the consensus among the development executives seems to be that there are some fantastically funny, very exciting, *very, very unique* talents here" (*Time*).
- "Residents of college basketball's *most unique* unincorporated village were in place yesterday afternoon, the day before their Blue Devils will face North Carolina" (*N.Y. Times*).

Arguably, our modern culture lacks and does not *want* absolutes, in intellectual life or in language. But stick with the uncomparable *unique*, and you may stand out as almost unique.

380. upbraid

verb

To reproach, to find fault, to criticize harshly.

I have never worked for fame or praise, and shall not feel their loss as I otherwise would. I have never for a moment lost sight of the humble life I was born to, its small environments, and the consequently little right I had to expect much of myself, and shall have the less to censure, or **upbraid**

> myself with for the failures I must see myself make.
>
> —Clara Barton
> Quoted in *Angel of the Battlefield*
> by Ishbel Ross (1956)

381. utilitarianism

noun

The ethical doctrine that actions are right because they are useful for the greatest number of people.

> A system of ethics according to which the rightness or wrongness of an action should be judged by its consequences. The goal of **utilitarian** ethics is to promote the greatest happiness for the greatest number. Jeremy Bentham, an English philosopher, was the founder of utilitarianism; John Stuart Mill was its best-known defender.
>
> —*The New Dictionary of Cultural Literacy*
> (3d ed. 2002)

382. vacuous

adjective

Empty, without content; lacking in intelligence or ideas; without purpose, idle.

> Television was not invented to make human beings **vacuous**, but is an emanation of their vacuity.
>
> —Malcolm Muggeridge
> "I Like Dwight"
> *Tread Softly for You Tread on My Jokes* (1966)

383. vapid

adjective

Having lost sparkling quality and flavor; insipid; flat; dull or tedious.

> A society in which everyone works is not necessarily a free society and may indeed be a slave society; on the other hand, a society in which there is widespread economic insecurity can turn freedom into a barren and **vapid** right for the millions of people.
>
> —Eleanor Roosevelt
> Quoted in *Eleanor: The Years Alone* by Joseph P. Lash (1972)

384. vehement

adjective

Very eager or urgent; zealous, ardent; characterized by rancor or anger; consisting of great exertion or energy.

> It is very natural for young men to be **vehement**, acrimonious and severe. For as they seldom comprehend at once all the consequences of a position, or perceive the difficulties by which cooler and more experienced reasoners are restrained from confidence, they form their conclusions with great precipitance. Seeing nothing that can darken or embarrass the question, they expect to find their own opinion universally prevalent, and are inclined to impute

> uncertainty and hesitation to want of honesty, rather than of knowledge.
>
> —Samuel Johnson
> *The Rambler,* May 14, 1751

385. venal, venial

adjective

Venal: willing to sell one's influence in return for a bribe; associated with bribery.

> From what we already know, . . . some churchmen had dealings with the SB [Polish Secret Police] for no other reason than that anyone in Poland who wanted a passport had to speak to the SB. Others, like Wieglus, signed agreements-to-cooperate; but there was a wide spectrum of cooperation, some of which did little or no harm. Still others constantly blabbed clerical gossip to the SB, which in the case of a former classmate of John Paul II, seems to have had more to do with ego than with any intent to harm the church. Others were **venal**, cooperating for money. And still others agreed to work with the SB because they were persuaded, somehow, that doing so would help liberalize the tight-ship church of Cardinal Wyszynski.
>
> —George Weigel
> "The Archbishop and the Secret Police"
> *WashingtonPost.com,* January 9, 2007

Venial: that may be pardoned or forgiven, a forgivable sin; trifling, not seriously wrong.

> Mortal Sin/Venial Sin. A distinction of sins that is stressed in the theology of the Roman Catholic Church. A mortal sin is serious enough to subject the sinner to damnation; willful murder, for instance, is considered a mortal sin. **Venial** sins are less serious.
>
> —*The New Dictionary of Cultural Literacy* (3d ed. 2002)

386. venerable

adjective

Meriting or commanding high esteem because of age or high dignity; impressive or interesting because of great age; hallowed or historic.

> Heaven and earth are grand; father and mother are **venerable**.
>
> —Chinese Proverb

387. vernacular

adjective

Concerning language, indigenous or native, as opposed to learned or literary; using plain, ordinary language; also pertaining to a style of architecture employing techniques, decorative arts, materials, etc., common to a particular place or time.

noun

Usually refers to the language of class or profession; the native speech of a place or region; also a style of architecture employing techniques, decorative arts, materials, etc., common to a particular place or time.

> You will find that the truth is often unpopular and the contest between agreeable fancy and disagreeable fact is unequal. For, in the **vernacular**, we Americans are suckers for good news.
>
> —Adlai E. Stevenson
> *New York Times*, June 9, 1958

388. vestige

noun

A visible trace, mark, or impression, of something absent, lost, or gone; a surviving evidence of a condition or practice.

> Most people with whom I talk, men and women even of some originality and genius, have their scheme of the universe all cut and dried,—very dry, I assure you, to hear, dry enough to burn, dry-rotted and powder-post, methinks,—which they set up between you and them in the shortest intercourse; an ancient and tottering frame with all its boards blown off. They do not walk without their bed. Some, to me, seemingly very unimportant and unsubstantial things and relations are for them everlastingly settled,—as Father, Son, and Holy Ghost, and the like. These are like the everlasting hills to them. But in all my wanderings I never came across the least **vestige** of authority for these things. They have not left so distinct a trace

> as the delicate flower of a remote geological period on the coal in my grate.
>
> —Henry David Thoreau
> *Walden* (1864)

389. vicarious

adjective

Suffered, done, received, or exercised in place of another, as in *vicarious punishment*; serving as a substitute; felt or enjoyed through imagination of experience of others, as in *a vicarious thrill.*

> Parents lend children their experience and a **vicarious** memory; children endow their parents with a **vicarious** immortality.
>
> —George Santayana
> "Reason in Society"
> *The Life of Reason* (1905–1906)

390. vicissitude

noun

A change, especially a complete change, of condition or circumstances, as of fortune; successive, alternating, or changing phases or conditions, as in *We have been friends through the vicissitudes of 39 years of marriage.*

> The greatest **vicissitude** of things amongst men is the **vicissitude** of sects and religions.
>
> —Francis Bacon
> *Of Vicissitude of Things*

391. vindicate

verb

To clear from accusation or suspicion; to provide justification for; to justify through argument; to get revenge.

> Psychology keeps trying to **vindicate** human nature. History keeps undermining the effort.
>
> —Mason Cooley
> *City Aphorisms* (1989)

392. vindictive

adjective

Inclined toward revenge, vengeful; showing a revengeful spirit.

> "That's why you were so much struck when I mentioned to Zossimov that Porfiry was inquiring for every one who had pledges!" Razumihin put in with obvious intention. This was really unbearable. Raskolnikov could not help glancing at him with a flash of **vindictive** anger in his black eyes, but immediately recollected himself.
>
> —Fyodor Dostoevsky
> *Crime and Punishment*

393. virulent

adjective

Intensely poisonous; in medicine, highly infective, as in *a virulent disease*; also, spitefully hostile.

> Every two years the American politics industry fills the airwaves with the most **virulent**, scurrilous, wall-to-wall character assassination of nearly every political practitioner in the country—and then declares itself puzzled that America has lost trust in its politicians.
>
> —Charles Krauthammer
> *Chicago Tribune*, October 28, 1994

394. visage

noun

The face, countenance, or look of a person; appearance, aspect, as in *the bleak visage of February.*

> He was small in stature, with a furrowed **visage**, which, as yet, could hardly be termed aged. There was a remarkable intelligence in his features, as of a person who had so cultivated his mental part that it could not fail to mould the physical to itself, and become manifest by unmistakable tokens. Although, by a seemingly careless arrangement of his heterogeneous garb, he had endeavoured to conceal or abate the peculiarity, it was sufficiently evident to Hester Prynne, that one of this man's shoulders rose higher than the other. Again, at the first instant of perceiving that thin **visage**, and the slight deformity of the figure, she pressed her infant to her bosom, with so convulsive a force that the poor babe

uttered another cry of pain. But the mother did not seem to hear it.

—Nathaniel Hawthorne
The Scarlet Letter (1850)

395. vitiate

verb

To impair the quality of, spoil; to debase, corrupt. In law, to make defective, as in *to vitiate a claim.*

> We do not draw the moral lessons we might from history. On the contrary, without care it may be used to **vitiate** our minds and to destroy our happiness. In history a great volume is unrolled for our instruction, drawing the materials of future wisdom from the past errors and infirmities of mankind. It may, in the perversion, serve for a magazine, furnishing offensive and defensive weapons for parties in church and state, and supplying the means of keeping alive, or reviving, dissensions and animosities, and adding fuel to civil fury. History consists, for the greater part, of the miseries brought upon the world by pride, ambition, avarice, revenge, lust, sedition, hypocrisy, ungoverned zeal, and all the train of disorderly appetites, which shake the public with the same.

—Edmund Burke
Reflections on the French Revolution (1790)

396. vituperation

noun

Censure or violent condemnation; verbal abuse, castigation.

> And as I grew into manhood, the newspapers rang on every side with disrespect for those in authority. Under the special dispensation of the liberty of the press, which was construed into the license of the press, no man was too high to escape editorial **vituperation** if his politics did not happen to suit the management, or if his action ran counter to what the proprietors believed it should be. It was not criticism of his acts, it was personal attack upon the official; whether supervisor, mayor, governor, or president, it mattered not.
>
> —Edward William Bok
> *The Americanization of Edward Bok* (1921)

397. vociferous

adjective

The quality of making a noisy and vehement outcry.

> In 2000 Mr. [Norman] Finkelstein, a vehement critic of Israel and the son of Holocaust survivors, published "The Holocaust Industry: Reflections on the Exploitation of Jewish Suffering," in which he argued that Jews in Israel and America have conspired to use the Holocaust to oppress the Palestinians and extort money

from Germany. Not surprisingly the book caused a sensation, leading to large sales and **vociferous** criticism.

—Patricia Cohen
"A Bitter Spat over Ideas,
Israel and Tenure"
New York Times, April 12, 2007

398. volition

noun

An act or exercise of will; the act of choosing, willing, or resolving.

> The good, by affinity, seek the good; the vile, by affinity, the vile. Thus of their own **volition**, souls proceed into heaven, into hell.
>
> —Ralph Waldo Emerson
> Address before Divinity College,
> Cambridge, Massachusetts, July 15, 1838
> Reprinted in *The Portable Emerson* (1946)

399. voracious

adjective

Eating with greediness or in very large quantities; very eager or avid, as in *a voracious reader.*

> The fish in neighboring streams and lakes are so **voracious**, it is said, that fishermen have to stand out of sight behind trees while baiting their hooks.
>
> —*The WPA Guide to Florida* (1939)

400. wanton

adjective

Done, used, or shown maliciously, without justification; done without motive or provocation, headstrong; without regard for right and wrong; sexually loose, lascivious; excessively luxurious.

> At this moment, my small daughter being out, I am acting as nurse to two wee guinea pigs, which she feels would not be safe save in the room with me—and if I can prevent it I do not intend to have **wanton** suffering inflicted on any creature.
>
> —Theodore Roosevelt
> *Theodore Roosevelt's Letters to His Children* (1919)

401. waive

verb

To relinquish, especially temporarily, as a right or claim; to refrain from claiming or insisting on; to put aside for a time, postpone, defer. In law, to relinquish a known right.

> "Well, even granting that, I don't think health has anything to do with goodness; of course, it's valuable to a great saint to be able to stand enormous strains, but this fad of popular preachers rising on their toes in simulated virility, bellowing that calisthenics will save the world—no, Burne, I can't go that."

> "Well, let's **waive** it—we won't get anywhere, and besides I haven't quite made up my mind about it myself. Now, here's something I do know—personal appearance has a lot to do with it."
>
> —F. Scott Fitzgerald
> *This Side of Paradise* (1920)

402. zealot

noun

One who espouses a cause or pursues an object in an immoderately partisan manner; a true believer.

> To attempt the destruction of our passions is the height of folly. What a noble aim is that of the **zealot** who tortures himself like a madman in order to desire nothing, love nothing, feel nothing, and who, if he succeeded, would end up a complete monster!
>
> —Denis Diderot
> *Philosophic Thoughts* (1746)

403. zeitgeist

noun

A German word, often appearing in the uppercase, which means "the spirit of the times" or "the general intellectual or temper characteristic of a particular period of time." These days, it's perfectly acceptable to write the word in the lowercase.

> As most critics and all professors of cultural

theory note, Madonna is nothing if not a skilled reader of the **zeitgeist**.

—"Techno 'rave' just the
same old Madonna"
Chicago Sun-Times, March 3, 1998

GrammaRight®

Clickable Help for Writers

Grammar.com

Ed Good, the author of *Vocabulary for Success* and *A Grammar Book for You and I ... Oops,* Me!, developed GrammaRight, a new clickable help system for all writers. Featured at Grammar.com, GrammaRight is a series of downloadable and fully searchable help files that can answer all your questions on grammar and writing. You can use it as a look-up system or as a training program to improve your writing immediately.

Here's the Home Page of GrammaRight. We encourage you to visit Grammar.com and learn more about this remarkable new system.

Welcome to GrammaRight

Click for the Introduction

Click a Button to Open a Section

Grammar & Writing Guide
- Answer questions on grammar and writing style.
- Use as a training program.

Grammatical Mistakes
- Learn from discussions of common grammatical mistakes.

Rules on Punctuation
- Learn how to use all punctuation marks.
- Study common problems on the use of periods, commas, semicolons, quotation marks, hyphens, colons, and dashes.

Click for the Help Section

Click for *New Yorker* Cartoons

Frequently Misspelled Words
- Look up 1,175 words that often escape the scrutiny of your spellchecker.

Problem Words
- Learn the differences between *affect* and *effect*, *principal* and *principle*, and 480 other troublemakers.

Erosion of Grammar
- Consider the author's lament on the deteriorating state of grammar in today's society.